Th

A Collection of Classic Magazine Articles on the History of Motor-Cycle Design

By

Various Authors

Copyright © 2011 Read Books Ltd.
This book is copyright and may not be
reproduced or copied in any way without
the express permission of the publisher in writing

British Library Cataloguing-in-Publication Data
A catalogue record for this book is available from
the British Library

Contents

Your Motor-Cycle. Archibald Williams…..............Page 1

The World of Wheels…..Page 9

Motor-Cycles of 1907…......................................Page 11

The Romance of the Motor-Cycle.
C. E. Hughes…...Page 17

The Case for the Motor-Cycle.
J. Pollock Castors…..Page 26

Motor-Cycle Notes. George A. Barnes…............Page 33

A Week-End on a Motor-Cycle.
Bernard Parsons…..Page 47

Light-Weight Motor-Cycles. W. G. McMinnies..Page 51

The Motor-Cycle of Today.
W. G. Mcminnies...Page 54

YOUR MOTOR-CYCLE

BY

ARCHIBALD WILLIAMS

PHOTOGRAPHS SPECIALLY TAKEN FOR "C. B. FRY'S MAGAZINE"

A COMBINATION of steel, rubber, and leather, weighing anything down to 15lbs., which enables a man to propel himself at all speeds up to fifty miles an hour is indeed a wonderful proof of the perfection to which the mechanical arts have been brought. But even more astonishing to the fair-minded thinker is the little petrol engine, scaling, with its accessories, less than half a hundredweight, which will move itself, a cycle, and a heavy human burden untiringly on the flat and uphill for hours together, covering a mile every three minutes, and asking in return but a whiff of spirit and a few drops of oil, with a spark of electricity thrown in.

The cycling community may congratulate itself that science and experiment combined enable us to have "a horse in a hat-box" attached to our machines, and to taste the delights of skimming over the road in a fashion that would have dazed the cyclist of last generation. Scoffers there are in plenty who can—and not without justice—lay finger on defects and drawbacks in motor-cycling. But that its advantages outweigh its disadvantages is self-evident from the rapidly increasing number of riders who are off with the first love of the pedal-driven machine, and on with the new love of the motor.

In the space of a short article it is impossible to range over the vast field covered by the details, varieties, and management of motor-cycles. The writer is, therefore, obliged to confine himself to such general considerations and advice as may be of use to the prospective purchaser or tyro.

The stoutest champion of the motor-cycle cannot honestly deny that, as a *class*, the petrol-motor is a "troublesome little beast" on occasions. A glance at the correspondence columns of motor journals will suffice to prove to the hilt that the ailments of these busy little engines are not a few; not to mention difficulties of transmission of power, etc. There are, of course, a favoured minority of riders who can give truthful witness to a wonderful freedom from trouble with their machines; but they *are* a very decided minority. That this should be so is not surprising, or, when properly viewed, a condemnation of the motor-cycle. Most riders are, prior to their motoring, quite ignorant of the management of self-actuated machinery, and of the primary facts of electricity. When, therefore, they take possession of an engine that makes any number of revolutions up to 2,500 a minute, and which depends for its vitality on a delicate electrical apparatus, they should not be surprised if sometimes the wheels refuse to go round. The motor, in spite of its rapid advance towards perfection, is not yet "fool-

A HEAVY-WEIGHT PEDALLESS CYCLE

A LIGHT-WEIGHT MOTOR, THE CLÉMENT-GARRARD, SCALING 80LBS.
(*From a photo supplied by Messrs. Garrard & Co.*)

proof." And even when it is perfect, something more than the pressing of a button will be needed to keep it in satisfactory motion. A railway locomotive is practically perfect, but how carefully its driver treats it!

There is no doubt that the motor-cycle of ten years hence will make its predecessor of to-day look antiquated enough. Meanwhile, we have some very good material to enjoy. Before purchasing we should decide what we really want our motor-cycle to do. Is it to be a riding-horse or a traction-engine? Is it to be used mainly in flat, undulating, or hilly country? Don't grumble if a motor quite strong enough to move you alone resents the attachment of a few friends to your coat-tails; and, on the other hand, don't complain if the engine which makes nothing of an extra passenger or two is not so handy, as regards weight and manageability, as one less powerful. Then, again, the avoirdupois of the rider must be considered; a ten-stone man will obviously not require as bulky an engine as one who scales half as much again.

There are several points about a motor-cycle which always find their way into motor-cycle conversation when a few kindred spirits are gathered together; and I consider that it will be worth while to at least glance at them. First, what shall be the weight of our cycle? That depends upon the purposes you

A PEDALLESS MOTOR-CYCLE WITH MAGNETO-IGNITION AND FREE CLUTCH

BEFORE STARTING ON A RIDE OVERHAUL THE NUTS CAREFULLY WITH A SPANNER, AND SEE THAT THE BRAKES ARE WORKING IN GOOD ORDER

mean to put it to. If it is to carry you alone, and you are not more than 11st. or 12st., two *real* horse-power will suffice for all ordinary conditions. If you are very heavy, or strongly object to walking any hills, or find that two is company on a ride and one is none, then you may with advantage add another horse-power. Let it be plainly understood, however, that the more powerful the machine is, the heavier it will be in proportion ; and that beyond 100lbs. every 10lbs. added renders it much less handy to move about. At the present time opinion seems to be on a kind of mental watershed, one slope of which inclines to " more power," and the other to " greater lightness." If I may venture a personal opinion, I should say that the motor-cycle of the future will develop, like the pedal-driven cycle, in the direction of lightness ; and that the makers will endeavour to increase the power of small engines, rather than add larger motors. When we have three horse-power safely installed in a 70lb. mount the motor-cycle *par excellence* will have " arrived." I think that the heavy machine is so prominent at present because the proper position of the motor-cycle has not yet been determined, and many riders desire their mounts to be more or less of a traction engine, from a very proper wish for sociability. By and bye the bicycle will become a solo instrument, and the cheapening small car obviate the " attachments " now so popular ; but the time is not yet.

Some heavy-weights are pedalless. It is certainly more comfortable to ride with the feet on the same plane than to have them splayed apart by the pedals. The argument of the no-pedal party is that if a pedalless machine breaks down it is too heavy to drive with the feet. On the other side it may with justice be urged that even a heavy mount can be propelled at a much faster rate on the flat or down hill with pedals than it could be without, and with very little more labour. So I advise you to stick to the pedals, and have one of them a "drop,"

DON'T ATTEMPT TO PASS A VEHICLE ON THE WRONG SIDE. IF YOU DO, YOU MAY GET DRIVEN IN AGAINST THE EDGE OF THE ROAD AND UPSET

BE VERY CAREFUL NOT TO CANT YOUR MOTOR-CYCLE FROM YOU WHEN WHEELING

such as is employed on the "Werner." In traffic pedals are often invaluable; and on a cold day they help you to keep your circulation going.

Now for carburettors. Shall we have a "spray" or a "surface" on our mount?

Many reams of paper have been covered to prove each form superior to the other; and the result is practically a drawn battle. A bad pattern of one. Given fine, dry weather and properly shaped pulleys the belt is satisfactory enough. But let rain descend and mud arise on to its surfaces, and there is trouble. Its rival, the chain, is undoubtedly coming into favour, and will probably supplant it —unless both be turned out by bevel gear and shafting. The chain will not betray you on a hill, or pull out its hook and lie snakily in the road behind you; though it does not give so sweet and elastic a drive as the leather, and necessitates the fixing of a clutch to free the engine. I certainly mean to give the chain a good trial, as my wrestlings

LOOKING BACK IS A DANGEROUS THING

either type is bad, and a good pattern of either type is good. I have used a "surface" for years, and, to tell the truth, have found it quite innocent of the crimes laid against its class. Its chief defects are that the vaporising chamber occupies space which with a "spray" is utilised for storing petrol; and that any petrol left in the chamber at the end of the run becomes stale. It has in its favour complete exemption from narrow passages which may be clogged by very minute particles of foreign matter—the *bête-noire* of the "spray."

One of the most troublesome things about a motor-cycle is the belt, if it have

A GOOD METHOD OF TOWING

with the belt, especially in its twisted days, have been many.

Now for that truly burning question of *ignition*. With accumulators I have suffered many things, and so has anybody else who has had long experience of them. They leak, they corrode, they short circuit, they become exhausted at inconvenient moments. No wonder that we motorists are looking for a perfect, self-contained mechanism to make its own electricity as the machine moves. I have tried a cycle driven by the Eisemann system of magneto-ignition, and I confess that I was pleasantly surprised by the effectiveness of the little dynamo, which weighs about as much as the two accumulators usually carried when touring. Even though many excellent patterns of accumulators are now made, I think that the fact that magneto-ignition is being applied to many cars is a strong point in favour of its being more largely used than it is on motor-cycles. Given a satisfactory dynamo the electrical bogey is effectively laid. I therefore suggest the following specification of a "solo" motor-cycle:—

Total weight, ready for the road, not exceeding 120lbs.

Ignition, magneto.

Power, 2 to 2¼ horse-power.

Saddle, large size, slung on N.A.B. spring pillar.

Pedals, one a swing.

Transmission, chain, with clutch for free engine.

Carburettor, either form.

Tyres, 2¼ins., with beaded edges.

Mudguards, 3ins. wide, carried well forward of front fork.

Wheels, 28ins.

Brakes, rim brakes, fore and aft, worked by hand.

THE CYCLIST'S BUGBEAR—THE "HANGER-ON"

Engine, vertical, in loop of frame: outside fly-wheel with heavy rim.

Valves, both mechanically operated, and as large as possible.

Strongly recommended features are: A folding stand attached to back axle; a change-speed gear for the pedals; a switch in left handle; a valve-lifter worked from the handlebars; a tap on cylinder head to squirt petrol through; the placing of lubricating pump on top of frame near the head.

The silencer should be of a good size, say four times the volume of the cylinder, and as noiseless as is compatible with absence of back-pressure; a cut-out may be fitted to turn the exhaust gases free into the air when climbing hills. The entire throttling of the exhaust should take place as it leaves the chamber, after expansion. The pop-popping of an inefficient silencer gets on the nerves towards the end of a long ride.

Before definitely purchasing a machine it is worth while to accustom oneself to motoring on a low-powered hireling. As soon as its various taps and levers are understood thoroughly the brand-new mount may be taken in hand. The novice must be careful how he holds his machine. If tipped away

AFTER THE DAY'S WORK

A—*Slip belt off pulley.* B.—*Raise back wheel on to stand.* C.—*Take out interrupter, to avoid leakage of electricity.* D.—*Take your lamps off and clean them out.* E.—*Shut off petrol or gas tap.*

5

from the body (see page 475) it may assert its weight and drag him down ignominiously on top. At corners he will do well to slow down, else he may make acquaintance with the ditch on the outside of the bend. It is also advisable for beginners not to look back, or ride "hands off," except on very good roads, as a small stone can work wonders with a cycle travelling at twenty miles an hour.

The horn should be used with judgment, warning being given in good time, especially when approaching a turn in the road. People do not yet appreciate the true speed of a motor-cycle, and hurry to drag their children off the road, as soon as the locomotive comes in sight; so that to wait until a few yards off before tootling naturally throws them into a panic. As silencers are improved the horn will be the more necessary.

In overtaking a vehicle *keep to your side.* You may think to steal past on the inside, and just as you come up the driver hears the motor and hurriedly "pulls in," nipping you nicely against the edge of the road, with no one to pity you. Another dangerous position that a motorist may find himself in is that of being pinched between two carts approaching each other from opposite directions. He hopes to dash in between; but the vehicles are closing in at the *sum* of their speeds, though each may be travelling quite slowly; and he discovers too late that he has grievously miscalculated. *When in doubt fall behind,* is here the golden rule.

If you wish to lend a pedalling companion a helping hand on no account have him on a string, or attached permanently in any way to your motor; at times it will be necessary for him to drop back; so rather tie something round your arm for him to catch hold of when everything is clear running. Don't take either of your hands from their work to catch hold of him.

The "hanger-on" is a nuisance on some of the main roads. He finds a fiendish delight in trying to keep his front wheel as near your back tyre as he possibly can; so giving you an uncomfortable feeling that if anything goes wrong with your mount he will be over you in a moment. If polite argument avails nothing, and your engine is not speedy enough to shake off the intruder forthwith, save the pace for the hills, and dash up them as fast as combined engines and pedals can carry you. After a stiff incline or two the motorless one becomes disheartened.

Before starting for a long ride, or once a week under any conditions, you should go carefully over the nuts and screws of a machine, to detect any looseness, since the failure of one might cause a serious accident. Especially attend to the nuts of the wheel spindles. When the ride is over prop the back wheel up on its stand; remove the belt (if you have one) from its pulleys; turn off the petrol or gas supply, and take out the interrupter plug, to avoid any possible leakage of electricity. The lamps should also be removed from their brackets, and the perished carbide shaken out.

HAVE A BIG LAMP AT THE HEAD AND A SMALLER ONE AT THE RIGHT OF THE FORK

THE WHITE BANDAGES ARE OVER THE PARTS OF THE BODY NEEDING MOST PROTECTION

A SMART FORE-CARRIAGE
(From a photo supplied by Messrs. Humber & Co.)

Talking of lamps, the night rider should be well provided with light. He will, of course, use acetylene burners; and it is well to reinforce the main headlight with a smaller lamp fixed fairly low on the forks, which will throw into prominence stones, stray half bricks, left on hills by careless carters, and other perilous objects. The light must be penetrating enough to illuminate the road at least as far ahead as the minimum checking distance of your brakes. In the pre-acetylene days, or rather nights, I had several narrow squeaks through insufficient light. On Sundays drunken men in their best black suits are very hard to distinguish.

At a very early stage in your experiences you will find that motoring is cold work as compared with "push-biking." You must wrap up well; overdress rather than underdress. I have pictorially indicated on page 477 those parts of the body that require most attention. The eyes should be glazed; the wrists protected with gauntlets or long gloves; the knees with thick stockings. Most important of all is the stomachic region, which is so sensitive to chills, and may advantageously be encircled by a cholera belt. Gaiters to the knees, thick

THE SIDE-BY-SIDE CARRIAGE—MOST CONVENIENT FOR CONVERSATION
(From a photo supplied by Messrs. Montgomery & Co.)

breeches, and a warm waterproof and flannel-lined coat with deep collar will enable you to keep quite comfortable. My experience has been that I have very seldom felt too heavily clad in any weather, as the rapid rush through the air counterbalances even a powerful sun; but I have often wished I had put on thicker clothing.

Attachments.—If solitary motoring palls, and your engine power is sufficient, you can choose between the trailer, the fore-carriage, and the side-carriage. The trailer is the most easily attached, but does little to hold the cycle up, and the passenger, while getting the mud and smell and noise from the cycle, is out of reach of conversation. The fore-carriage attachment, by converting the whole into a tricycle, can stand on its own wheels, and is more sociable, but often over-heats the engine, which it largely screens from the air-draught. The side-carriage is, from a social point of view, the most desirable contrivance of the three, but it occupies more of the road, and offers the greatest resistance to the air, as the riders are not travelling in the same line. For my own part I hold that a fore-carriage, frame and wheels, should be a *permanent* part of the machine; be fitted with brakes — properly compensated—on both of the front wheels, in addition to that on the driving wheel; and have a two-speed gear for the engine. The basket-work should be easily removable when a passenger is not to be carried.

A good word may be said for the newer types of motor-tricycle with two rear wheels. One great advantage with this class of machine is that the chain or belt, as the case may be, is well out of the way of mud. Another, that the drive is taken by two tyres. It will be interesting to see whether the motor-tricycle, in its more modern forms, will not have another lease of life, and regain some of the popularity lost by its noisy, gear-driven predecessor.

Whatever mount be chosen the rider should keep these four cardinal points of management in mind: careful lubrication; clean terminals; good compression; and a plentiful supply of electricity. Under the third head it may be remarked that the twisting of the

"YOUTH IN THE (GOVERNESS) CAR"
(*From a photo supplied by Messrs. Singer & Co.*)

rings is a frequent cause of loss of power. It will repay you to have a circular hole filed at the slot of each ring, and a small pin screwed into the piston of such a size as to loosely fit the hole. The slots in a three-ringed piston must be 120degs. apart. If the exhaust valve requires frequent grinding-in—which is very bad for it—you may be sure that the engine is overheating; and that such excess of heat is caused by an insufficient or badly timed lift of the exhaust valve, a choking silencer, a bad carburettor, or by the engine pulley being too small in proportion to that on the driving wheel. Space forbids me to discuss here electrical details, tyres, etc.; but as every motorist should thoroughly understand the mechanical principles of his engine throughout, I strongly recommend him to study one of the valuable handbooks which explain these matters in full. A fit piece of parting advice is: Every rider should drive cautiously for his own sake, and considerately for the sake of other users of the road. If the increase of motor-cycles leads to an epidemic of scorching, such as seized a certain class of pedal cyclists ten years ago, and has been more recently noticeable among car drivers—then the sport may fall on evil times.

8

THE WORLD OF WHEELS.

A WALK THROUGH THE OLYMPIA CYCLE AND MOTOR-CYCLE SHOW.

WITH the printer's devil worrying for copy, the "walk" through Olympia resolved itself into a sprint, or at least that hurried kind of zig-zag scamper which one makes when hurrying through a crowd. How tiresome slow crowds are! That is to say, walking crowds. Is it any wonder we all seek so naturally for increased speed in locomotion? Normally I should like to saunter through Olympia, and make circuit after circuit at slow pace, so great and numerous are the attractions. But needs must when the printer's devil drives, and so I must give a few hurried impressions.

In pedal cycles there was a brave show, all at wonderfully moderate prices, and looking more fascinating than ever. We are past the day of revolutionary change in the foot-driven machine, and we must fain look for little refinements, and novelties in fitting and equipment. But for the presence of the motor-cycle we might, perhaps, find more striking alterations brought about in the ordinary cycles, if only for the sake of change. Fortunately this is not necessary, and in the modern high grade, variable geared machine we have a cycle which is as near finality in its class as we need hope for.

Turning to the motor-cycles it is surprising to find what an immense influence has been wrought by fixing a little motor to a cycle. The whole character of the machine has undergone a big development, and from year to year we are getting more remarkable and ingenious contrivances, so that every possible requirement is met.

It is the tendency of the age to travel quickly, and conserve energy. The motor-car answers both these purposes, but it fails in the other vital essential of doing it very cheaply. Once you travel on four wheels the cost goes up astonishingly, and so it is that the two-wheeler and the three-wheeler motor-cycles fill a great need for the thousands of people who cannot afford the more expensive pastime.

For 1912, motor-cycles come in greater variety than ever, and there is no lack of machines at really moderate prices. Of course there are absurd people who are waiting for the £10 motor-cycle, and needless to say it will not come about in their time—or in any other time. A very cheap motor-cycle could be made to-day, but it would be a very costly thing for the man who purchased it. You must have good work and good material in the power-driven cycle, and it is comforting to find that no firms of repute are trying to do impossibilities.

There are many novelties to be noted in the new designs. Smaller powered machines are more numerous, and we are getting nearer to the ideal of the light, simple, and reliable machine suitable for the average man or woman. Variable gears are meeting with general favour, and here again we find all-round improvement. The engines on the whole are smoother running, less noisy, and better hill climbers. Ease of adjustment has been carefully studied, tyres can be attended to more readily, and altogether the light motor-cycle is more fitted for the ordinary cyclist than heretofore.

We have a distinct class in the more powerful machines intended for heavy loads, and side-car work, and here again improvements are numerous, the sum total being shown in increased reliability. Then as a development of this class we have various interesting machines of the passenger carrying type which bring us close up to the small motor-car in various respects, and yet are quite distinctive. Generally, there has been an increase in engine efficiency; and many of the new light motors are marvellously powerful.

Of the individual stands it is pretty certain that the Triumph display was one of the most popular. They showed a fine range of push cycles, and nine motor-cycles. Several of these had the Triumph free engine clutch, which allows the machine to be started like a car, and brought to a standstill in traffic with the engine running. Improvements are noticeable in the ignition, carburation, and the valves, the latter being very quiet in action. The machines are beautiful models in every respect, and I must defer a detailed description until later, so numerous are their good points.

The "Handy Hobarts," as usual, excited much interest. The 2½ h.p. single

The World of Wheels.

cylinder is remarkable value at £38; and there is a very smart lady's model, with three-speed gear. For fast work, with or without side-car, the 3½ h.p. Hobart is a splendid specimen. All the machines are noted for their simplicity and ingenuity.

A striking exhibit was made by the Birmingham Small Arms Company. Their "All Black" push cycle is commendable for the man who does not want to bother about keeping the plating clean. In motor-cycles they showed their "Tourist Trophy" model, with and without pedalling gear, a free engine model, and a two-speed free engine model. The free wheel hub is a new and excellent feature, and the cantilever spring forks make the B.S.A. machines very strong and distinctive.

Rudge motor-cycles will be very popular next year, so attractive are the new models. Two machines were shown fitted with the new Rudge multi-speed gear, and the free engine clutch and pedal starting gear excited much favourable comment. The engines are splendid jobs. In the push cycles celluloid covering is fitted to many of the plated parts to preserve their appearance.

The Swift motor-cycle created a very good impression by its neatness and up-to-dateness. It is of the free engine type with pedals, and is a very smart little mount.

Rex machines were in strong array, and included single and twin cylinder engines, side-cars, and also water-cooled engine models. The de luxe machines have two-speed gears and free engines. A splendid display, of interest to every class of motor-cyclist.

The famous F.N. machines were to be seen in the four cylinder 2¼ h.p. and 5-6 h.p. types, the former a two-speed, and shaft-driven machine, the latter having a four cylinder engine like the former, and pump lubrication, and in fact as near an approach to a motor-car engine as one can see. The F.N. Company also make a motor-tricycle which has met with great favour.

Four N.S.U. models are made for next season, all with the firm's loop frame. They are of 2 h.p. single cylinder, 3 h.p. twin cylinder, 3½ h.p. single cylinder, and 6 h.p.

The Alldays machine for 1912 has a 3½ h.p. free engine, and a neat two-speed gear. The power plant is very well installed.

The purchaser of a Singer machine can select from the standard roadster, tourist trophy, free engine, and two-speed models, in both heavyweight and lightweight types. They are uncommonly smart machines, full of good features, and noted for their smart running and reliability.

A good programme has been prepared by the Rover Company for next year, and their touring machines are most carefully designed to meet the requirements of the amateur rider. The grouping of the parts is admirable, and in appearance and design the 3½ h.p. Rover never fails to win attention for itself.

Of particular interest is the Moto-Reve machine for 1912. This remarkably light and simple machine has come through the present season with flying colours, and for 1912 the models are still further refined.

Space prevents me from giving details of the many other machines on view, but I must draw special attention to the new Humber machines. Their new Duo-car is a most interesting machine of the passenger carrying type, and is really a miniature car. Extraordinary speeds were recently shown by the 2¾ Humber at Brooklands; and all the Humbers are noted for their smooth running on the roads—up hill as well as down. The distinctive Indian machines with their chain drive, free engine, forced lubrication and two-speed gear were also prominent at the show.

Three main types of Premiers can be had for next season, and these are to be seen in fourteen different models according to the various requirements. Included in them is a very nice model for ladies. For hard work the 3¾ h.p. Premier with variable gear will take a lot of beating.

The ingenious little Motosacoche for 1912 has attracted much notice, following on its wide success in this year. It can now be had fitted with change speed gear, and this lightweight machine with 2½ h.p. engine, and the new gear can climb Sunrising Hill without pedal assistance. The stroke of the engine has been increased, and this will add to its power.

Royal Enfields in 2¾ h.p., 2½ h.p. lightweight, and 6 h.p. side-car machine make aroused much attention. The 2½ h.p. is suitable for ladies, and is a delightful model. The New Hudson Cycle Company also made a fine display of their 2¾ h.p. and 3½ h.p. models, with three speed gear.

Dunlop tyres and motor-cycle belts, Palmer tyres in various types; the new Clincher, non-skid, the Hutchinson, Continental, and many other types; Bradbury side-cars, many new designs by Mills and Fulford, the Clyno side-car, various three-wheelers, made with a wealth of accessories by Lucas, Dunhill's, and all the other firms, a really splendid show.

Motor-Cycles of 1907

AN EXPLANATION OF THE TECHNICAL TERMS USED

MOTOR-CYCLE is a comprehensive term, which includes *bicycles, tricycles,* and even *quadricycles,* and in some cases, as in the case of the *quadricycles,* the machine very nearly approaches what might be called a motor-car. When a motor-cycle has two seats, one behind the other, the front seat being upholstered, and the rear seat being more in the nature of a bicycle saddle, it is known as a *tri-car.* In this case, of course, it has three wheels, the rear driving wheel and two front steering wheels. When this front part is detachable, and can be fitted to a bicycle frame—that is to say, the two front steering wheels and the upholstered front seat can be made to take the place of the front wheel of a motor-bicycle—the detachment complete is generally known as a *fore-car.*

A *quadricycle* is a type of motor-cycle having four wheels.

The *engines* of motor-cycles are in all cases *internal combustion engines,* that is to say, they consume their fuel inside the engine itself. There are no steam motor-cycles on the market, though there may be in the future.

The fuel used is a distillation from petroleum, and is known as *petrol;* for this reason these engines are generally known as *petrol engines.* On motor-cycles there are two kinds, *air cooled* and *water cooled.* The water-cooled engine becomes necessary when the power is high, such as is required for *tri-cars* and the heavier two-seated motor-cycles, but it is very seldom used on motor-bicycles, which almost exclusively use *air-cooled engines.*

The difference between the air-cooled and the water-cooled engine lies in the fact that the former *radiates* the heat away by means of *radiating ribs* around the *cylinder,* while the latter radiates the heat through the medium of the *water jacket,* which is practically a water reservoir forming part of the cylinder casing, and entirely surrounding it. When the water-cooled engine is used the water in this *water jacket* must be circulated through the *radiator,* which is an appliance for radiating away the heat contained in the water taken up from the cylinders. The *radiator* is placed in some position where it will get the full force of the draught caused by the rapid forward motion of the machine.

In order to burn the fuel inside the cylinder so as to cause the expansion necessary to create the power we must mix it with air, and the appliance which is used for this purpose is known as a *carburetter,* because it carburates the mixture, or in other words transfers it into hydro-carbon, with the proper proportion of air to ensure its combustion. That part of the cylinder in which this combustion takes place is called the *combustion chamber,* and is always situated at the head or top of the *cylinder.* Carburetters are divided into two classes, the *spray carburetter,* in which the suction of the engine is used to cause the spirit to be sprayed through a fine aperture and so mixed with the requisite proportion of air, and the *surface carburetter,* in which the air is drawn through or over a body of petrol and becomes saturated with the petrol vapour. The latter type is now seldom used, but is found on the older motor-cycles. It is wonderfully economical, and suffers from no derangement, being free from any mechanical or moving appliances.

The expansion caused by the combustion forces out of the

cylinder a moving *piston,* and from this motion is communicated to the *crank-shaft* by a *connecting rod.*

The *crank-shaft* is a rotating member, which carries the fly-wheel, and is the first point from which the power is taken off and transmitted to the road driving wheels.

In order to ignite the fuel in the cylinder of the engine we use some form of electric spark, and the appliance in which this spark is formed is known as the *sparking plug.* This consists of two points, one electrically insulated from the other, across which the current of electricity jumps at exactly the right moment.

The source of the electricity is the *accumulator,* which is an appliance for storing up electrical energy. The current from the accumulator is known as the *low-tension current,* but as the low-tension current would be useless for forming the spark across the points of the *sparking plug* it has to be transferred into a *high-tension current* by means of an *induction coil,* always spoken of amongst motor drivers as the *coil.*

The high-tension current formed in the *coil* is the current which passes across the points of the *sparking plug* and ignites the charge in the *combustion chamber.*

In order that the spark shall occur just at the right moment the machine is fitted with an appliance driven by the engine, which makes contact in the circuit of the low-tension electrical current at precisely the right time. This is known as the *contact maker.*

When a contact maker is used a *trembler* on the coil is necessitated. When a similar appliance to the contact maker, but one which breaks the contact instead of making it, is used, the trembler on the coil is not necessary, and this appliance is known as the *contact breaker.* The appliance for breaking contact used in magneto ignition is also known as a *contact breaker.*

In many motor-cycles the spark across the points of the sparking plug is caused by a high-tension current of electricity generated in the *magneto machine,* loosely known as the *magneto.* This machine has to be mechanically driven by the engine, and the current which it generates is transformed into a *high-tension current,* as we have explained, either by an extraneous *induction coil* or by an induction coil actually incorporated in the mechanism of the magneto itself. This form of magneto ignition is known as *high-tension magneto ignition.*

There is another method of igniting the gas charge by means of a magneto machine in which the low-tension current only is used, and in this case there has to be a mechanical *contact breaker* acting inside the cylinder itself. This contact breaker is often described as the *sparker,* and the system of ignition is known as the *low-tension magneto.* It is, however, very rarely used in connection with motor-cycles.

In the majority of motor-cycles the power is transmitted from the engine to the back wheels directly by means of a belt or a chain. This is generally spoken of as the *transmission.* The simplest transmission is by means of a *V-pulley* on the engine crank-shaft, and a *belt* of V-section, which exactly fits it, and which drives on to a bigger V-pulley attached to the rim or the spokes of the rear wheel.

Sometimes a chain transmission is used, and is loosely spoken of as the *chain drive.* At other times a more direct drive or transmission is arranged by means of shaft and bevel wheels, and this is called a *bevel drive.*

In bicycles, as a rule, the engine is started by pedalling the machine along, the usual bicycle pedals and a chain being provided with a free *wheel clutch* on the rear wheel, and the engine always being directly geared to the road wheel. When we come to the heavier machines, such as the tri-car or the fore-car, we have to use some system of change-speed gear, so that when ascending steep gradients the engine may run at a higher speed relatively to the cycle. The mechanism which gives us this change of gear is known as a *change-speed gear*.

Some motor-cycles are so arranged that the engine may be started before the machine is mounted, and afterwards put into engagement with the transmission mechanism. For this purpose there is provided what is known as a *clutch*, which takes its name from the fact that it clutches one part of the transmission to the other. On account of the fact that in the majority of cases the engine is permanently geared to the rear wheel, this mechanism is generally described as a *free engine clutch*, because it allows of the engine being made free of the transmission.

In some cases the two-speed gear is fitted in the back hub or on a drum mounted alongside the back hub. These gears, by reason of the arrangement of the different gear wheels, are known as *epicyclic gears*.

Some motor-cycles are fitted with engines having two cylinders, and are known as *twin-cylinder* machines.

R. J. MECREDY.

SPECIFICATIONS OF THE BEST MOTOR-CYCLES

THE J.A.P. TANDEM.—3 horse-power three-cylinder J.A.P. air-cooled engine; transmission by J.A.P. roller worm drive and disc clutch direct from engine to driving wheel; Longuemare carburetter; ignition, single coil and high-tension distributer, two-way switch, J.A.P. plugs; lubrication by automatic sight-feed drip lubricators; patent two-speed gear. Price 120 guineas.—John A. Prestwich & Co., 1, Lansdowne Road, Tottenham, London, N.

THE MATCHLESS.—6 horse-power twin-cylinder J.A.P. engine; Brown & Barlow carburetter with throttle and air-valves; Simms-Bosch high-tension magneto ignition (or coils and accumulators); Wata Wata belt; two brakes (Bowden, and "Matchless" back-pedalling). Price, with accumulator ignition, £50; with magneto ignition, £55.—H. Collier & Sons, Herbert Road, Plumstead.

THE CLARENDON.—3 horse-power Clarendon engine, the distinctive feature of which is the outside pulley bearing—this takes the full driving strain of the belt, which actually runs between two bearings; Togo belt; Lithanode or Pfluger accumulators; trembler coil; tank carries petrol sufficient for 140 miles. Price £37 10s.; magneto high-tension ignition £5 10s. extra; spring forks £1 extra.—Hammon & Smith, Ltd., Dale Street, Coventry.

13

THE ANGLIAN.—Fitted with a De Dion 2¾ horse-power engine; a single-cylinder motor of 3½ horse-power can be fitted without extra charge; guaranteed to climb any hill, being fitted with the Anglian patent two-speed gear, which provides a free engine and a foot-operated clutch; Wata Wata belt; all mechanism except carburetter out of sight. Price £50.—Anglian Motor Co., Ltd., Newgate Street, Beccles, and 72, Brompton Road, London, S.W.

THE ARMADALE TRI-CAR.—8-10 horse-power Stevens engine; Longuemare carburetter; high-speed trembler coil; friction drive; eight forward speeds and two in reverse; front brake operated by foot pedal, back by side lever; inclined pillar steering, geared and irreversible; Bowden system of control throughout; friction clutch operated by foot pedal; the radiator is behind front seat, circulation Thermo-Syphon; upholstered in best pegamoid. Price 135 guineas. —The Armadale Motors, Ltd., 319, Trinity Road, Wandsworth Common, London, S.W.

THE COB.—Fitted with Phœnix 2 horse-power or 2¾ horse-power Minerva motor; mechanically operated inlet and exhaust valves; Longuemare carburetter; ignition, Bassee Michel coil or Simms-Bosch high-tension magneto; large special Phœnix silencer; chain-driven by Hans Renold motor chain; two-speed gear, containing clutch and free engine enabling hand-starting; Phœnix exhaust valve lifter, combined with spring current interrupter, enabling full control and any graduation of pace. Price, 2 horse-power, £45; 2¾ horse-power, £50; five guineas extra if fitted with Simms-Bosch magneto system.—Phœnix Motors, Ltd., Blundell Street, Caledonian Road, London, N.

THE RIP.—White & Poppe 3½ horse-power engine; trembler coil; two 15 A.H. "Rip" accumulators; Brown and Barlow or Longuemare carburetter; automatic sight-drip feed lubricator; Bowden valve lifter; springs on both wheels allowing 4½in. action; front brake and back brake controlled by foot lever; belt 1in. V-section. Price forty-five guineas; magneto five guineas extra.—The "Rip" Motor Manufacturing Company, 14, Leytonstone Road, Stratford, London, E.

THE ANTOINE.—Two-cylinder 4½-5 horse-power engine; accumulator or Simms-Bosch ignition; automatic "Antoine" carburetter; special unbreakable fork; long handlebars; band-brake back and front; 1in. V-section belt transmission; the machine weighs 165lbs. Price, with accumulator ignition, £34 8s.; with Simms-Bosch high-tension magneto ignition, £42 10s.—W. G. Haywood & Co., Ltd., 56, High Street, Bloomsbury, London, W.C.

PHELON & MOORE.—The machine made by this firm has foot-rests to replace pedals; fitted with engine of their own manufacture; spray carburetter; petrol capacity for one hundred miles; two accumulators; two-speed transmission, high 4-9, low 8-4. Price, if fitted with accumulator and coil ignition, 2¾ horse-power, £47 10s.; 3½ horse-power, £50; if fitted with high-tension magneto ignition, 2¾ horse-power, £50; 3½ horse-power, £52 10s.—Phelon & Moore, Valley Road, Cleckheaton.

BROWN'S MIDGET BI-CAR.—Fitted with Fafnir engine; girder front forks; two brakes; Bowden exhaust lift; handlebar switch; two accumulators. The feature of these machines is that they are built very low, the top of saddle being only 30ins. from the ground. Price, 3 horsepower, twenty-eight guineas; 3½ horse-power, £31.—J. T. Brown, 18, King's Road, Reading.

THE TRIUMPH.—New Triumph ball-bearing engine, giving 3 horse-power at 1,500 revolutions; ignition, special coil with low current consumption, two Pfluger accumulators and Triumph rapid-break contact breaker; New Triumph cut-out and exhaust valve lifter, operated from inverted lever; patent spring forks. Price, with accumulator ignition, £43.—Triumph Cycle Co., Ltd., Coventry.

THE "VINDEC SPECIAL."—Engine made by the famous Fabrique Nationale (F.N.); magneto ignition; fitted with Truffault suspension forks; two-speed gear hub; new design of handlebar, enabling rider to sit well back. Price, 3½ horsepower, £55.—South British Trading Co., Ltd., 13-15, Wilson Street, Finsbury, London, E.C.

THE BROWN.—Single cylinder; cylinder and combustion head cast in one piece; mechanically operated inlet and exhaust valves; high-tension ignition; can also be fitted with Simms-Bosch magneto ignition; model H. Longuemare carburetter; famous "Duco-Flex" belt fitted; two powerful brakes. Price, 2¾ horse-power, £34; 3½ horse-power, £37.—Brown Brothers, Ltd., 22-30, Great Eastern Street, London, E.C.

Roc Military Model. — 4 horse-power M.O.I.V. engine; Simms-Bosch high-tension magneto ignition; large Longuemare carburetter; Wata Wata belt. The outstanding feature is the free-engine device, which allows the engine to be started by rotating the rear axle. Wheels 26in., fitted with Clincher A Won tyres; the machine is built very low, enabling the rider to have both feet on the ground when sitting on the saddle. Price forty-five guineas.—A. W. Wall, Ltd., Roc Works, Guildford.

The F.N. — 4½ horse-power four-cylinder engine, air-cooled, greatly improved oiling system; automatic inlet valves; F.N. type of carburetter, entirely automatic; Simms-Bosch magneto ignition with patent F.N. current distributer; bevel gear transmission, enclosed in water and dust-proof casings, elastic coupling in motor fly-wheel; strong back-pedalling expansion drum brake, also back-wheel rim-brake. Price £50.—The F.N. Motor Agency, 106, Great Portland Street, London, W.

The Onaway.—5 horse-power engine, either the twin-cylinder Kelecom, or the Bercley, with two vertical cylinders side by side and having air-draught between; Kelecom or Longuemare carburetter; transmission by 1in. continental rubber belt; "Onaway" handlebar control by means of thumb-slides; friction clutch, actuated by same lever applying brake on back wheel; spring forks; ignition, G.L. non-trembler coil, and two Lithanode accumulators, or Simms-Bosch high-tension fitted to Bercley engine. Price forty-six guineas.—The Onaway Motor Engineering Company, 42a, St. Albans Road, Watford, Herts.

The Rex. — 3¾ horse-power engine; Rex vibrationless frame design; Rex cylinder, spring forks, engine cradle, silent silencer, patent foot brake, push and pull lever control, switch and exhaust lifter, and belt; the commutator and carburetter are encased; the management is very simple. Price twenty-five guineas.—The Rex Motor Manufacturing Co., Ltd., Coventry.

F. CHASE BREAKING THE FIFTY MILE RECORD. HIS TIME WAS 1HR. 7MINS. 57⅘SECS.

THE ROMANCE OF THE MOTOR-CYCLE

BY

C. E. HUGHES

ILLUSTRATED FROM PHOTOGRAPHS BY RUSSELL & SONS

THE FIRST MOTOR PACING MACHINE BUILT AND USED IN ENGLAND
In use to pace A. A. Chase.

IF the words which head this article have at first sight something of the appearance of a paradox—and doubtless they will have for not a few persons who read them—that, perhaps, constitutes a very good reason for writing them, for it proves that there are misconceptions in regard to motor-cycles which require to be explained away. There is nothing at all paradoxical in connecting romance with automobilism. The horseless carriage and the cycle that goes without pedal-work may be the last products of an age which is grinding itself into a state of sound common sense by means of machinery. In a limited sense they are, but there is romance about them all the same. Consider the matter. What made the motor what it is to-day? Or first, perhaps, consider the thing itself; what is it? A noisy, snorting, dangerous engine, you will say. Likely enough it will smell a little, and with it all it is infernally expensive. Well, good friend, let us not fall out over mere words. One has known in one's time motor-cars that are noisy, and motor-cars that snort, and some, doubtless, that are dangerous; and some that smell. So we will agree thus far, because it is ill arguing with generalities. But in the matter of that little after-thought about the expense—for it was an after-thought—let us talk awhile. The motor-car has been hitherto, and is, very largely for the man of means. You will say that the modest man doesn't get much of a look in, and we may imagine, perhaps, that you, good friend, you yourself, are figuring in your own mind as the modest man. Well now, modest man, you say that motors are noisy, dangerous, odious, and odoriferous, and the rest of it; and you say they are expensive. Tell us, then, what kind of a price you would care to pay for this amazingly troublesome article. You must have a notion, or you wouldn't call it expensive; you would call it dear at any price. You would declare roundly that you wouldn't accept one as a gift. You don't say that, and one fancies that you don't mean it. What you do mean is this—let us have it put bluntly for you—that the motor-car and you are much in the relative positions of the fox and the grapes. And, dear modest man, you are wrong. You would really like a motor. You would like to be able to get about quickly and easily. You would love to enjoy the inimitable sensation, the unique sensation of speed. And you think you can't afford it because you put it down at some hundreds of pounds at the least, with something in addition for a motor-man. You think! Have you thought of a motor-cycle? That is the thing which will solve the difficulty for you. It is like a pair of steps to enable you to reach those very delicious sour

THE START FOR A SPEED-TEST ON THE CRYSTAL PALACE TRACK

MOTOR-CYCLISTS WEIGHING-OUT BEFORE A RACE

grapes. That is the motor-cycle to-day. Not much romance there! Well, that is because we are looking at results. There is not much romance about wireless telegraphy. It is marvellous, but it is too coldly scientific to be romantic. Yet there is romance in the consideration of how wireless messages used to be sent. Think of the semaphore waving its black arms on hill-tops, and you will have rare stories ready-made. That is just an instance, but the truth of it is universal. In the present there is never any romance. "Romance is dead" has been the cry of generations. But the hard facts of to-day are the romance of to-morrow, and what we now call romance was once the last word in development. The romance of the motor-cycle, then, is the romance of development—the old tale of "Excelsior," the striving for improvement. All pioneers are really of the world of romance.

How, then, has the motor-cycle reached its present stage of development? The process has been much the same as with motor-cars—speed trials, races. The Gordon Bennett race is to many people simply an orgy of speed. It means nothing more to them than that a certain number of men have been selected to sit in machinery-fitted iron boxes, which may very possibly serve them as winding-sheets. Motor-racing means a good deal more than that. There is danger in it, of course. The drivers take their lives in their hands. So also do explorers entering a virgin country. But when an explorer comes successfully back from a dangerous expedition he has some definite result to show for it. He has found out something. So with the motor racer. He has learned precisely what each part of his machine will do—the exact value to the whole scheme of each particular nut and rivet. And that means a lot to the man who drives a motor-car in the street, though he may not think it. The extraordinary development of motor-cars during the last few years is almost entirely due to experiment in racing.

The same work is going forward in connection with motor-cycles. Speed and reliability trials have done much to increase their efficiency. We are regarding the matter here from the point of view of the motor-cycle, so this is not the place to debate the question of whether the paced cycle race gives the truest test of ability. Mr. Leon Meredith and Mr. G. A. Olley, both of whom hold enviable and well-known records, have both expressed the opinion that road-racing, provided always that the conditions are the same for each competitor, is beyond question the fairest method of disclosing a man's real capabilities. And that view is undoubtedly the one which must commend itself to the ordinary lay mind, for, obviously, so much depends on the pacing motor in a track race, that the best man need not necessarily always win. But, sporting considerations aside, this fact of the large dependence of the cyclist on the motor-man in front of him is the thing which has—or should have—most interest for our friend the modest man, who has his eye on that tempting bunch of grapes, the sensation of speed. For the ingenuity which is brought to the manufacture of suitable machines for pacing, and the experience which is gained by runs on the track, are the agents working to the end that our excellent modest friend may have a reliable and serviceable machine for the road.

Pacing motors are almost as carefully dealt with as racehorses before they run in a race. The limit usually allowed on English tracks is a 150lb. machine of not more than 2½ horse-power, and the cycles are carefully tested and weighed before they are passed for entry. The somewhat restricted margin thus given has put a good many wits to work, for it is no very simple matter to produce a good, strong-going machine which does not exceed the weight limit. A rather notable achievement in this line is the two-cylinder machine made by the Minerva Company, one of which was ridden by the Belgian M. Olieslargers, who paced Mr. Olley in his recent race for the world's championship.

The pacing motors join the race after the first lap, starting on the top of the banking, and allowing their followers gradually to drop in behind them. The pace is then regulated by the cyclist, who gives his directions—faster or slower—as he thinks fit.

The effect of the pacing machine on the cyclist following is very considerable. As to what one may call its moral effect, Arthur Chase, recently the world's cycling champion, once compared it rather happily to that of a band leading a body of men. As the music, so to say, carries the men along with it, so the motor-cycle seems to assume the responsibility of shaping the course, and to leave the man behind free to devote his attention to the actual working of his machine. Additional assistance is given by the wind shield. This is placed at the rear of the motor, and protects the cyclist's legs from the rush of wind. It measures 18ins. by 24ins., or often less, and covers only the lower part of the following bicycle. The rider of the motor himself acts, of course, as a wind screen for the upper part, and some idea of the advantage he confers thereby may be gathered from the fact that the slightest movement of his arm from its regular position frequently makes a draught sufficient to put a visible check on the cyclist behind. On the Continent and in America very much larger wind screens are seen on tracks. So large are they, indeed, that the cyclist is practically borne along by the force of pneumatic suction which they generate. Some of the remarkable records made in America and elsewhere by Robert Walthour have been made with the help of these big shields, which reduce the need for skill to a minimum, though in fairness it must be said that Walthour has shown himself capable of remarkable feats without them.

A FINAL OVERHAUL BEFORE THE START

GOING FOR THE HOUR

A broad notion of the differences in speed without pacing, with pacing, and with an ordinary wind shield may be obtained by an estimate of miles per hour. An unpaced cyclist who can do twenty-five miles an hour can do easily about thirty-five paced, and forty if his pacer carries a wind shield.

Each cyclist in a race paced by motors generally has two pacing machines, so that a change may be made in case of accident. For although one machine may go through a race, it is not safe to rely upon one. If one of the machines breaks down, or is in any way disabled — a puncture, say — the rider signals to his waiting companion, who comes upon the track and takes up the work. This is on many occasions a feat demanding some neatness of execution, particularly when the competitors are running close together. Generally speaking, the second motor runs alongside the first, and the cyclist changes at a word from one to the other, but there are times when no rule of action will serve. Motor-cycles have been known to collapse and stop almost dead, and the cyclist will be lucky if he can avoid running right on top of the motor-man. The pacer, therefore, has to take a good deal of responsibility. He must do his best to anticipate accidents, and to effect them with the least possible danger, if

THE FIRST LAP IN THE RACE
The Crystal Palace track will allow a motor-cycle to travel safely at a speed of thirty to thirty-five miles an hour. The Copenhagen track will allow any rate up to sixty miles an hour.

THE ROMANCE OF THE MOTOR-CYCLE

G. A. OLLEY MOTOR-PACED IN THE 100 KILOMETRE RACE
Showing the wind shield which protects the legs of the cyclist from the rush of wind.

they are inevitable. But, of course, the pacer is not concerned with all the accidents that take place on a cycle track. He is not responsible, for example, for those that result from riding at a speed which is too great for the track. The maximum speed at which a cycle may travel on a track is determined by the angle at which the track is banked. The Crystal Palace track will allow a cycle to travel safely at a speed of thirty to thirty-five miles an hour. Anything above that is dangerous, and it is something to its credit that no fatal accident has ever taken place on it. The Copenhagen track will allow practically any speed up to sixty miles an hour. On account of its weight the motor-cycle is able to keep its footing, so to say, on the track at a speed which would be impossible for an ordinary cycle, so it is obvious that the question of speed must lie with the cyclist. The pace of the pair, like that of an army, must be that of the slowest unit.

One of the worst accidents which has happened to Leon Meredith was due probably to this difference between the possible speeds of the bicycle and the motor. It was on the Palace track, and Meredith, getting along in fine form, had urged his pacer to a speed of something like forty-three miles an hour, when he arrived at the bend at one end of the course and discovered that he had not enough room to allow his machine to take the natural curve which the speed demanded. As a result he had the track equivalent of a side-slip. He turned about five somersaults, left behind some valuable portions of his clothing and anatomy, and was laid up for a month. Such an accident is naturally not in the least the matter of the motor-man, any more than was the puncture which brought Olley over in the world's championship. It can only be attributed to excessive zeal on the part of the cyclist. That, in fact, is Meredith's chief sensation when riding a race. He has no sort of anxiety. He merely feels that he has got to win, come what may.

Olley is very much the same. The competitive spirit seems to subdue in him any sense of the danger of the work. The real mental strain, curiously enough, comes after the event, and he confesses that he seldom sleeps well on the night following a great race in which he has taken part. Chase, one of the very few crack riders who have won a world's professional championship, claims to enjoy the most comfortable and pleasant moments of his life when he is following his pacer, and all is going well. But he has had several bad falls on the Palace track—two of them were on exactly the same spot—and he admits that there are times when that spot, rushing towards him as he is flying round, brings

ROBERT WALTHOUR, OF AMERICA, WHO HAS MADE MANY RECORDS MOTOR-PACED

just the slightest sensation of unhappiness. Well, it is intelligible. One never likes meeting one's enemies, even at forty miles an hour.

No article on motor-cycling, however slight, could close without some reference to Fred Chase, who has paced his brother Arthur to victory in all his races and record rides, for the two Chases, by applying the experience gained in their respective lines, have probably done more to bring motoring within reach of the modest man than anyone else in England.

LEON MEREDITH, WINNER OF THE 100 KILOMETRE MOTOR-PACED RACE
Meredith covered the distance in the record time of 1hr. 35mins. 0¼sec.

THE CASE FOR THE MOTOR BICYCLE

WRITTEN BY J. POLLOCK CASTORS

THE following pages are devoted to a comparative and illustrated review of a number of the most popular motor-bicycles now before the public. It is impossible, in the space available, to expatiate at any length on the details of each individual machine, but a *résumé* of this kind should serve a purpose of its own by picking out interesting facts, and gathering into a small compass some of the information otherwise obtainable only through the perusal of a string of catalogues, advertisements, and notices in the motoring press.

We open with

THE LIGHT-WEIGHT,

designed to meet the requirements of a certain class of riders. It has its virtues and its shortcomings as well, for the simple reason that, though lightness is eminently desirable, the cutting down of weight precludes the use of certain refinements which make for comfort, and entails a reduction of power and speed. Whether the light-weight is or is not the type to be chosen by any particular person must depend largely on the purposes for which it will be used, and the quality and contours of the roads over which it will most generally have to travel. Other conditions would also influence a choice. For instance, if the only available storage place is at the top of a flight of steps, a ninety-pounder would be very feasible, and a heavy "twin" quite out of court.

It may be freely admitted that some of the light-weights on the market are of high quality, and do their work well. To notice a few of them:—

THE MOTOSACOCHE has established itself as a thoroughly smart and reliable little machine. The mechanism throughout is carefully designed and manufactured. Either coil and accumulator or magneto ignition is fitted. There is a very neat arrangement for clipping an accumulator in place and

The Moto-Reve.

making contact without using screw terminals. Side plates, bent out in front to direct air on to the cylinder head, completely enclose the tank, engine, and ignition apparatus. The power of the engine is set down by the makers at 1½ horse-power, but judging

The Motosacoche.

The Case for the Motor-Bicycle

by the cylinder dimensions and the working speed this would appear to be an under-estimate, and 2 horse-power nearer the actual output. That the Motosacoche is a "stayer" has been proved by long reliability trials. It scales about 85lbs., and has found favour with many people who would refuse to have anything to do with the heavy-weight.

The Rex.

THE MOTO-RÊVE is another promising example of the light class. Its two-cylinder engine—the smallest of the kind made, we should imagine—gives it a special interest. The cylinders are of 2in. bore and $2\frac{1}{2}$in. stroke. The fittings include "Druid" spring forks, foot-rests, magneto, and handlebar control, compression cocks on the cylinder heads, petrol gauge in the tank, and petrol filter. The round belt, once fashionable for light-weights, has been replaced by a specially flexible V belt. The tyres are proper motor-cycle tyres. This machine has attained a speed of $37\frac{1}{4}$ miles per hour on the road, and won several medals for all-round performances. Weight about 90lbs. Rim brakes.

THE REX light-weight is of $2\frac{1}{4}$ horse-power ($3\frac{1}{2}$ horse-power according to R.A.C. rating). Has a specially designed duplex frame, enabling the rider to reach the ground easily with his feet. Automatic inlet valve. Magneto ignition. Has 2in. motor tyres. Weight, 90lbs. Foot brake on belt pulley rim; hand brake to front wheel. Price 25 guineas, giving very good value.

THE N.S.U. light-weight—$1\frac{1}{4}$ horse-power; 60 by 70mm. engine; Simms-Bosch magneto ignition. Weight 80lbs. Price, with spring forks, £36 7s.

Coming to the heavier class of machines one notices the growing popularity of the change-speed gear. The difficulty of starting a fixed gear heavy-weight up a slight incline, and even on the flat, has turned the maker's attention to the free, handle-started engine and clutch transmission; while the exigencies of hill-climbing, negotiating traffic, and side-car work have called for a two-speed gear. When the belt drive is retained the gear, of the epicyclic type, is usually found in the hub.

A very effective two-speed and free-engine mechanism is incorporated into THE ROC, a low-built, pedalless machine. The spindle of the driving wheel is "live," that is to say, it revolves in ball bearings on the fork-ends, and is driven by the belt pulley. On it turns the hub of the wheel. The belt pulley is connected up to the hub through an epicyclic gear-box, which is either held stationary, to give the low speed, or locked to the belt pulley, to give the high or solid drive. When the gear-box is entirely unrestrained, the normal or free-engine condition, for starting-up, wheeling, or coasting is obtained. The gear is exceedingly strong, and very suitable for attachment to any make of motor-cycle. The Roc engine includes ball bearings on the crank-shaft. "Druid" forks are fitted. Brakes, metal-to-metal contracting, magneto ignition. The tanks, unusually large, hold two gallons of petrol—sufficient for a 200-mile run. Two models are made—the 4 horse-power, single-cylinder standard military model; and the 5-6 horse-power twin. Prices, inclusive of magneto and two-speed gear, 48 and 55 guineas

The Vindec Special Model G.

27

The Case for the Motor-Bicycle

respectively. For side-car work the Roc cannot be beaten.

THE REX is notable for its spring-fork device, very resilient cantilever seat, expanding brakes, and twin tyres, and the ball bearings in the engine at the big end of the piston-rod as well as on the crank-shaft. The Roc clutch has been adopted in combination with a two-speed pedal-operated gear embodying much the same principles as the Roc, but placed on the right instead of on the belt side of the wheel. The fitting of twin tyres to the back wheel minimises side-slip, and reduces puncture troubles, as one tyre is sufficient to do all the work till its punctured fellow can be repaired. Rex machines have won prizes and medals galore in competitions of all kinds, and rank with the best.

THE VINDEC SPECIAL, made by the South British Trading Company, of Finsbury, also has a large number of

The Phänomen.

victories to its credit. Two models—3½ horse-power, single; and 5 horse-power, "twin." This firm has retained the automatic inlet valve, but gone for magneto ignition, spring forks—the "Truffault Suspension," quite rigid laterally—and pedals. The two-speed gear hub fitted to their machines resembles somewhat in outward appearance a magnified Humber Cordner three-speed for ordinary cycles. To obtain the high or "solid" gear, two dog clutches are allowed to engage; while the low gear transmits motion through the ordinary epicyclic train, the drum of which is gripped by a band brake. All 1908 Vindecs are fitted with an adjustable pulley, to give direct gears ranging from 3¾ to 1 and 5½ to 1.

THE PHÄNOMEN hails from Germany.

The Colliers' "Matchless," 3½ h.p.

Its two-speed "Nala" hub is operated by a single lever and transmits power through metal-to-metal friction clutches. The pedals are connected to the belt pulley, so that when the gear is in the neutral position the engine may be started-up by giving one of them a half turn with the foot. This is an interesting feature. The application of the rear band brake cuts off the ignition current. Spring forks; magneto; automatic inlet; back mudguard hinged, for tyre repairs. Cooling fan, driven off the crank spindle, fitted to two-speed machines. Models—3 horse-power, 3½ horse-power (single cylinder); 4 horse-power, 6 horse-power (twin).

THE MATCHLESS (H. Collier & Sons, Plumstead) has some fine performances to its credit, notably the winning of the Tourist Trophy Race in the Isle of Man last summer at an average rate of about 40 miles an hour—a 3½ horse-power machine in this case; and the covering of 56¼ miles in an hour. The "Jap" engines adopted by the firm are famous for their speed and reliability. The two-speed gear, fitted to both 3½ horse-power and 6 horse-power models, has leather-faced clutches which engage very quietly. The 3½ horse-power machine weighs only 140lbs., and the more powerful twin 160lbs., so that they are decidedly "handy" mounts. Magneto ignition;

"Brown" 3½-h.p. two-speed.

28

The Case for the Motor-Bicycle

The "N.S.U." two-speed gear.

belt drive; spring frame. A 120lb. 2½ horse-power model with two-speed gear is included in Messrs. Colliers' list.

The Brown motor-cycles introduce us to the chain drive and the two-speed gear on the crank-shaft of the motor. The gear is on the Crypto principle, with direct drive on the top speed, and low speed working through an epicyclic train, both engaged by friction. The transmission is by chain from the engine to a counter-shaft, and thence by chain to the driving wheel. Models—3½ horse-power and 5 horse-power (twin). For fixed-gear cycles the belt drive is retained. Magneto ignition; spring forks.

The N.S.U. motor-cycles also employ a two-speed mounted on the crank-shaft, but here the transmission is by belt. The reduction of gear is 35 per cent. Magneto ignition; spring forks. Models —2¼, 3, 3½, 3¾ horse-power singles; 4, 5½, and 6 horse-power twins. The engine has two novel features—the mechanical operation of the inlet valve by a long-rod gear, and a small pipe leading from the exhaust to the jacket of the carburetter through a tap to regulate the heating effect.

Messrs. Phelon & Moore, of Cleckheaton, Yorks, make a speciality of a pedalless, two-speed, chain-driven motor-cycle. In this case the gear is simplicity itself. On the end of the crank-shaft are two sprockets of different sizes which drive two other sprockets on the counter-shaft. A third sprocket on the counter-shaft passes on the drive to the road wheel. Three chains are used. The change of gear is effected by bringing one or other of what we may call the primary chain drives into action by means of a fric-

The "Zenith," with "Gradua" gear.

tional expanding ring inside the counter-shaft. A single lever gives either speed and free engine. The crank-shaft chains are enclosed in a metal box, to prevent oil-throwing. Interesting features of the engine are the manner of mounting it in a four-tube cradle, and a device for giving half-compression and ease in starting-up. The advance of the spark automatically restores the full compression. Models — 2¾, and 3½ horse-power. The "Vapp" carburetter fitted also has several novel details.

The Zenette (Zenith Motors, Ltd.) takes a line of its own with a variable pulley, and a frame so divided that the rider is practically isolated from road shocks. The expanding pulley has

The Phelon & Moore.

29

The Case for the Motor-Bicycle

The "Bat," with spring frame.

We may now turn to some of the prominent single-gear motors. The recent mention of spring frames at once suggests that doughty machine—

THE BAT, of 3½, 6-7, or 7-9 horse-power, as you please. The *specialité* of this cycle is the supplementary frame carrying the saddle and foot-rests, and supported by springs and ball bearings. This frame and the Bat ball-bearing

usually been associated with a movable jockey to take up the slack as the belt is allowed to sink deeper into the groove. The Zenette gets over the difficulty in a more ingenious manner, by a worm shaft, which simultaneously expands the pulley and decreases the distance between the driving wheel centre and the engine, and *vice versâ*, so that the belt tension is constant. When the pulley is full open the belt "bottoms" on a loose ring, and a free engine is obtained. The rider, having started the engine with a handle, turns a wheel on the end of the worm-shaft and gradually closes the pulley till the engine takes on the "load." Mr. F. W. Barnes, the inventor of the "Gradua" gear, deserves considerable credit for his ingenuity in producing a device which has proved itself very efficient in practice. The machine—fitted with a 3½ horse-power Fafnir engine and footboards—is an extremely comfortable one to ride. The same firm makes the "Zenith Bi-car," peculiar for the absence of any front forks. It has a free engine and two-speed gear, and, as its name implies, suggests a car in several constructional points.

The Minerva.

spring forks, adjustable to any weight, give a luxuriously comfortable seat. The firm fits "Jap" engines, and also the J.A.P. patent automatic sight-feed lubricator to the crank chamber. Other details—magneto fitted in tank and driven by gear; two foot-applied band-brakes; long, horizontal levers at side

The Quadrant.

of tank to give very exact control. Bat machines are quite "top-hole."

THE TRIUMPH machines have established a reputation for splendid workmanship, neat design, and fine pulling power. Their particular type of spring fork is about the best on the market. In many a hard fight and test the Triumph has come off with flying colours. Few riders who have used one of these machines would exchange it

The Triumph, 3½ h.p.

30

The Case for the Motor-Bicycle

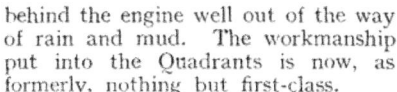

The Lloyd.

for another make. The latest model (3½ horse-power), which is fitted with two-speed gear, gives excellent results. A two-cylinder Triumph has not yet been produced, as the company pins its faith to the "single." The magneto is chain-driven. The stand which forms part of the equipment is extremely rigid, and is attached to the forks in such a way as not to interfere with the removal of the rear wheel.

THE MINERVA is an old friend, but vastly altered since the 1¼ horse-power days. It has fallen into line as regards magneto ignition and spring forks: and its engine power has risen to 8 horse-power in the largest twin. In spite of many rivals it still manages to hold its own, showing good workmanship at moderate prices.

THE QUADRANT is another of the old-timers brought thoroughly up to date. The Quadrant was one of the first to adopt spring forks, and also one of the last to abandon the surface carburetter. As a hill-climber the Quadrant has proved one of the best. The latest models (3½ horse-power) have mechanical inlet to the engine, magneto ignition, and a throttle which simultaneously increases or decreases the air and gas supplies. Pedals are retained, and aluminium rubber-faced footplates provided. The magneto is placed behind the engine well out of the way of rain and mud. The workmanship put into the Quadrants is now, as formerly, nothing but first-class.

LLOYD motor-cycles, designated by the letters "L.M.C.," may be mentioned next, since Mr. W. J. Lloyd was once connected with the Quadrant Company, as designer of their machines. Points—magneto lubricated from the engine; reversible exhaust tappit; metal tool cupboard under petrol tank; improved stand, independent of rear axle; low frame; weight complete 163lbs.

THE DIAMOND motor-cycles (Victoria Trading Company) are of 2½, 3½, and 4 horse-power. The last is a twin-cylinder. All models except the 2¼ horse-power, which sells at £26 10s., are fitted with a type of spring forks

Ladies' "Motosacoche."

which gives plenty of resilience but keeps the wheel quite rigid laterally. Low frame, long wheel-base and handle-bars, Bosch high-tension ignition, back-pedalling band-brake on rear wheel, and Bowden horse-shoe on front. There is a large tool-case in the frame under the saddle. Carrier and stand included.

The four-cylinder "F.N." motor-bicycle practically monopolises the market in this particular type of machine. The latest model is one of 4½ horse-power. A very sweet and flexible drive is obtained by the use of so many cylinders, and, owing to the frequency of the exhaust, the engine is a very silent one, purring instead of popping like the single-cylinder. The transmission is effected by means

The "F.N." 4½ h.p., four-cylinder, gear-driven motor-cycle.

The Case for the Motor-Bicycle

of gearing. A pinion at the rear of the crank-shaft meshes with a pinion on a long rod running on ball bearings inside the right chain-stay, which has on its other end a bevel pinion operating a large bevel attached to the hub of the driving wheel. The gear is entirely enclosed and inaccessible to mud and dust—a feature greatly appreciated by riders of the " F.N." This form of transmission is admirably suited for a four-cylinder engine, giving a power stroke every half revolution, and so rendering the act of starting free from the jerks which the gear would be subjected to by a single, or even two, cylinder engine. The " F.N." has obtained a wide vogue on the Continent, and many of its kind are to be seen on English roads. It is well made throughout. Magneto ignition with distributor.

LADIES' MACHINES

Opinions vary very widely among the manufacturers as to the prospects of motor-cycling gaining favour with the ladies. Some assert that nervousness, lack of sufficient muscular power, and the unsuitability of the skirt, will keep the ladies out of the saddle, though they may look favourably upon a seat in the side-car or fore-carriage. On the other hand one firm writes : " Motor-cycling for women will come, but not yet. It would well repay a firm of good repute, with the funds and the patience to permit of their awaiting the harvest, to design a lady's motor-cycle of about 2 horse-power, light, low, long, and handy, and to exploit it vigorously."

At the present time there are two good ladies' machines on the market : the " Motosacoche " (illustrated), and the " Matchless." The second of these has a 2½ horse-power Jap engine, two-speed gear, spring forks and spring frame, and weighs about 100lbs. The makers guarantee it, if fitted with two-speed gear, to climb any hill with rideable surface in England. The " Motosacoche " is designed with a large loop in the frame, enabling a skirt to be worn with comfort. Its magneto ignition removes the dirtiness of accumulators, while its lightness (80lbs.) makes it easily handled by any woman of ordinary strength.

The Diamond, 2¼ h.p.

MOTOR CYCLE NOTES

OUTLOOK OF THE NEW SEASON.
IS THE PUSH-BIKE DOOMED?

By GEORGE A. BARNES

[*We have no greater authority in Great Britain on motor-cycling matters than Mr. George A. Barnes, and his lucid and practical articles in the various leading motoring journals are read with the greatest interest and avidity by all motoring men. Once again has this notable record-breaker and expert been prevailed upon to express his views on current features of the sport for the benefit of "Fry's Magazine" readers.*]

LAST year I went out of my way to make what some considered a bold statement in regard to the nature and construction of the motor-cycle of the future. It was that the day of the heavy and high-powered machine was over, and that in its place we should witness an adoption of handy, light-weight, and less powered machines. Some thought I was speaking a deal in advance, but the subject had been well considered by me from all points of view, and the expression was the outcome of close study and analytical reasoning.

Only the other day very strong confirmation came directly to my notice, for in conversation with the manager of one of the best-known Paris racing tracks—a man who watches, apart from speed events and pacing matches, the wider developments of motoring—he assured me that the adoption of the light-weight machine was now phenomenally in evidence abroad, and that he himself, for his pleasure jaunts and road travelling, had abandoned the old type for the new. At home the same fact is in evidence, for hundreds of riders have discarded their awkward and almost unmanageable heavy mounts for the more ideal, comfortable, and really luxurious light-weights, in whose favour I have always unreservedly spoken.

※ ※ ※

THE cycling fraternity all want to motor. Yet they have been afraid of taking to the huge, ponderous, and costly machines hitherto in vogue. Fancy being landed twenty miles from nowhere with a broken-down motor-cycle which feels like a ton when you are pushing it along! This of itself has hitherto kept a number of people away from motor-cycles, let alone the question of cost, which naturally debars those whose finances are limited and who have to measure their pleasures out with a careful and sparing hand.

Yet these conditions are now all changed, for there is a machine on the market to-day which places the enjoyment of motor-cycling within the reach of practically everyone.

There is no need for me to apologise for referring to the "Motosacoche." Hundreds, like myself, have been literally charmed with its merits and virtues. Here you have a motor attachment which every owner of a roadster cycle can instantaneously affix to his bike and transform it into a speedy, reliable, and comfortable motor-cycle capable of taking you along at a rate of thirty miles an hour if desired. The man who invented the "Motosacoche" has proved himself to be a public benefactor. Personally, I feel more than indebted to him, for since first taking to the "Motosacoche" I have, for road purposes, in the words of the Pears' soap enthusiast, "used no other."

※ ※ ※

HERE we are in the early days of spring, with the glowing prospects of the season before us. If we adhere to our push-bikes we shall still be casting envious eyes on those who pass us by on motor-propelled machines. But why remain old-fashioned and stagnant when you now have the opportunity of becoming a fully fledged motorist at little cost and practically no trouble?

I cannot here describe at length just what the "Motosacoche" arrangement is; suffice it to say that it consists of a complete petrol motor and attachments which you can, in less than five minutes, fix on to your ordinary bike and transform it into an elegant and up-to-date motor-cycle. Its appearance is the most elegant you could desire. There is perfect control, entire absence of vibration, and a luxury of travelling which, once experienced, cannot be done without in the future.

When at the Stanley Show last year I was not surprised to see that the stand of the "Motosacoche" people was the centre of attraction. Neither was I surprised to hear that the business they did there was a record one. People were simply tumbling over each other in their keenness and anxiety to inspect it, and all seemed pleased beyond measure at its capabilities and appearance.

It could not well be otherwise, for from every point of the compass it appeals to riders. Here you have a machine hardly heavier than an ordinary bike. One you can manage with the greatest ease; one you can take any-where and everywhere; one that is economical in a remarkable degree, and which fulfils every wish and desire of the rider.

※ ※ ※

IF you once see or use a "Motosacoche" you would be as keen as I am, and it has gratified me very much to notice that the enterprising proprietors have adopted a very sensible plan in order to bring their machine to everyone's notice. They have expressed their willingness to let any *bona-fide* cyclist have a free trial run upon it at any time or place convenient. All that one has to do is to notify them of such a desire by writing to the Motosacoche British Office, H. and A. Dufaux, Ltd., at 65, Holborn Viaduct, London, E.C.

our article, namely, that not only in shooting, but in all sports and games requiring aim, and depending upon correctness of aim, a correct understanding of the theory of the master-eye and its function in aiming explains many common failures. To us it seems that the general theory expounded in our article is sound to the point of being incontestable. But one or two correspondents have raised debatable points.

* * *

The Question of Natural Eye
ONE correspondent is rather contemptible of all theory. He wants to know how it is that the most skilful exponents in such pursuits as rifle-shooting, golf, cricket, and so on, have achieved their success without knowing anything at all about the theory of the master-eye and the vertical plane of aim. (The latter point refers to the original and new theory set forth in our article, that the foundation of aiming consists in the attempt to get master-eye, implement, and object, not into the same straight line, but into the same vertical plane.) But surely the answer to this point is clear enough. A man can do a thing absolutely in accordance with theory and yet know nothing about correct theory at all. In fact, he succeeds because, without knowing it, he conforms with theory, and is, in fact, an example of correct practice in accordance with correct theory. Theory and practice, by the way, so far from being opposed, are different aspects of the same thing; a thing cannot be correct in theory but not in practice, unless the theory itself is defective for some reason or other, generally by reason of leaving essential data out of consideration. In any case, it is not the perfectly successful exponent, guiltless of theory, whom theory most concerns, but the wholly or partially unsuccessful exponent; for the latter it is who wants to know why he fails and how, and theory helps him to find and correct his fault.

* * *

The Ambiguity of the word Theory
THE word theory is often used in connection with games of skill, and it leads to much misunderstanding and fruitless argument, because it is ambiguous; it has two meanings which are often confused. First it means hypothesis or assumption. When people form theories concerning comets, the sun, the cause of earthquakes, and so on, they imagine a great many things which may or may not exist. Such theories are really complicated hypotheses—they may be wild and absurd; they may be correct but not capable of proof. Hence theory is used (mere theory, as we say) to mean supposition and speculation, and is opposed to knowledge founded on fact. There used to be two theories or hypotheses of electricity, neither of which is substantiated by anything we actually know of electricity. Secondly, theory means something quite different from supposition or speculation, namely, the general knowledge or science corresponding with a particular art or practice. It implies the possession of a complete series of general and accurate laws, but in no way distinguishes them from accurate knowledge in general. Thus, for instance, the theory of the steam engine does not mean anything hypothetical or merely supposititious, but the general laws derived from exact observation and experiment of the action of steam, of heat, of friction, of expansion of metal, together with the various relevant parts of abstract and applied mathematics, and so on.

Thus it is that theory may mean either mere hypothesis, as distinguished from fact, or scientific knowledge, as distinguished from practice. In treating of a subject like rifle-shooting, theory may mean a merely hypothetical, and perhaps wildly incorrect, explanation of some fact the causes of which we do not happen to know; or it may mean the scientific general laws which govern all correct aiming, and which we know to be perfectly valid. When we talk of the theory of shooting, of back-play in cricket, of " eye on the ball " in golf, we do not mean, or ought not to mean, mere hypothesis, but (so far as it goes) scientific knowledge. But the mistake is often made of calling a mere hypothesis theory, and then treating this kind of theory as if it were the other kind of theory, namely, scientific knowledge. It is theory in the sense of scientific knowledge that assists in improving defective practice.

* * *

The Question of what the term "Eye" means
BUT, to return, another correspondent suggests that the term "eye" as commonly used in reference to games of physical skill, really means, not merely

[Continued on page 200.]

accurate vision and accurate ocular judgment, but the complicated system of eyesight, nervous impulse, muscular action, and so on. " A man," he writes, " is said to have a good eye when he has a natural knack of making good shots at things, whether with an implement such as a cricket bat, or with a missile such as a cricket ball ; and seeing accurately is only one part of making a good shot ; quite as important a part is the accurate working of the limbs in obedience to the dictates of the brain, in which process the question of personal error intervenes." All this is true enough, but our article dealt not with " eye," but " the eye " in sport, and was intentionally limited to that part of " eye " which concerns eye-sight.

" Personal error " is a kindred and connected subject of much interest. Every cricketer knows that "his eye is out " and his " personal error " greater when his liver is out of order. There is nothing like a chill on the liver to reduce a skilful batsman to impotence and small scores. This, however, does not alter the fact that seeing accurately with the master-eye is the primary condition of every kind of aiming. If from any cause the master-eye is out of action the whole mechanism of aiming is out of gear.

* * *

"Eye" a Wide Term THERE are some gifted individuals who preserve a " good eye " in spite of taking extreme liberties with their health. For instance, there is the case of a first-class cricket professional, well known, and indeed famous, some fifteen years ago, who scored a wonderful seventy-seven on a bad wicket when he was far from fit to make a consecutive statement, and who, when hauled up and reprimanded, wanted to know "which of you gents would ha' done it sober ? " But for most people " good eye " mainly is the result of a maximum of fitness and good condition. Tom Cribb, the famous prize-fighter, who trained by walking, and walked mostly with a gun, declared that he could shoot nine times as straight after a month's training, and used his " eye " somewhat as a meritometer of his condition.

* * *

The Great Value of Walking Exercise THE other day I heard from Mr. Joe Clayton, the old Salford harrier, who has trained many famous runners, and latterly football teams, and is the best professional trainer I have met. He writes in cordial support of an article of mine in praise of walking as the exercise of exercises. He refers to a passage in " Boxiana," descriptive of Tom Cribb's method of training, which says : " He (Cribb) gained more in strength and wind by his journeys to the Highlands than by any other part of his training process." The context shows that the pugilist's pursuits in Scotland consisted mainly of walking. We have long ago abandoned the lines followed by athletes of the days of the prize-fighters. But the ancient belief in the efficacy of walking should never become obsolete. Perhaps the walking, which was right, neutralised much which was wrong in the ancient regimen.

* * *

Training of Tom Cribb THE details of Cribb's training are interesting. For one great occasion, on which he turned out a marvel of fitness according to accounts, he was in training eleven weeks, nine of which he spent at Urg in Scotland. Before he began to train he weighed 16st., " and from his mode of living in London, and the confinement of a crowded city, he had become corpulent, big-bellied, full of gross humours and short-breathed, and it was with difficulty he could walk ten miles." He started getting into condition by dosing himself with medicine. For two weeks he walked about as he pleased, " and generally traversed the woods with a fowling-piece in his hands ; the reports of his musket resounded everywhere through the groves and the hollows of that delightful place, to the great terror of the magpies and wood-pigeons." That is to say, Tom spent a fortnight in living the healthy life he ought always to have lived. Then he began real training by walking ten to twelve miles a day, and soon increased this to eighteen or twenty. Every morning and evening he ran a quarter-mile at top speed. At the end of five weeks he weighed 14st. 9lbs. In the next month he reduced himself to 13st. 5lbs., which was his " fighting weight." When fit he could do thirty miles a day with ease ; in fact he walked from Urg to Mar Lodge in two days, a distance of sixty miles, without distress. What else he did besides walking the account does not specify, but evidently he made walking his staple

THE SPORTSMAN'S VIEW POINT

exercise, and based his condition upon it. Nowadays, we should consider thirty miles a day a mad amount of work in training.

* * *

The Risks of the Rider

SOME time ago we had in this magazine an informative article on the risks run by those who ride in steeplechases; and the author mentioned that Mr. Hugh Nugent, who was killed in a fall at Ostend jumping a two-foot privet fence, was firmly of the opinion that, " the bigger the fences the safer they were, and he looked upon Liverpool and Punchestown—the biggest countries in the world—as the two ideal countries to ride over."

Writing, not on falls in steeplechases, but all kinds of falls, Mr. W. H. Ogilvie, in the *Badminton*, concludes that in general the risks of injury from falls in riding are much over-rated. " It may be accepted," he says, " that the worst falls are taken over low, trappy, or insecure fences. The clean, stiff, and high timber brings about a much smaller number of accidents, even when attempted upon horses which have hitherto had no reputation as jumpers."

In the hunting field bad falls rarely occur owing to the size of obstacles; they usually result from something unseen, such as a drain or ditch, or tree-stump, which throws out the horse in taking-off or in landing; the obstacle itself is more or less subsidiary. The common statement, however, that all horses can jump, and jump much better than riders' nerves allow, is well enough if we also bear in mind that it makes all the difference whether a horse is fresh or tired. A tired horse labours in jumping as in galloping, and cannot jump as he would if fresh.

It is interesting to learn that the best horsemen of the Queensland cattle camps, or the best cowboy riders of Montana, consider the greatest risk in riding to be in mounting a " bad " horse. But there is a difference in kind between cowboys riding, with a " bad " horse included, and riding across country either hunting or steeplechasing; for the former case would be a case of " rough riding," where the intractability of a horse is the chief difficulty understood, whereas the latter is concerned with the performances which horse and man together attempt with unanimity.

A NEW "SWIFT" VENTURE

A New Venture

THE SWIFT CYCLE COMPANY has entered the publishing arena with a very bright little journal, which performs the double task of advertising the Swift cycles and giving the cycling public some good disquisitions on cycling topics in general. Looking through the first two monthly issues, and noting the contributors, one meets the names of well-known cyclo-journalists : Messrs. C. H. Larette, John Urry, H. W. Bartleet, and H. S. Griffin, who may be relied upon to furnish palatable fare. Mr. Bartleet gives, in the February number, some useful hints as to the formation of a cycling club, after making the following very sensible remarks, among others : " I think many of those enthusiasts who identify themselves with the establishment of new (and generally small) organisations, would be better advised if they threw in their lot with older and already established clubs. It will be conceded that the officials of clubs which have been running for some time have acquired the necessary experience which the promoters of a new club must lack—they have probably made their mistakes and profited by them, they know what pitfalls to avoid, and how to surmount the difficulties which arise from time to time; so that to those unattached cyclists who are on the look-out for a suitable club I would say, look round and see if you cannot find a club in your neighbourhood composed of men of your own social position, and carrying out a programme which coincides with your tastes and abilities. Only if such a club cannot be found would I recommend the starting of a new body."

Clubs apart, companionship doubles the pleasure of cycling. In fact, the purely constitutional ride taken *solus* is little if any better than the solitary grind on foot. Some people might consider it even more of a labour of duty. It is, in truth, much more difficult now than it was a decade ago to find a *fidus Achates* willing to put in a Saturday afternoon or a week-end with you on wheels; so when found he should be cultivated. What with motoring and golf many once keen cyclists have lapsed from the ranks, and 'tis hard to lure them back again on to the pedals. Nor is it simply a question of counter-attractions. The dust raised by the motor-car has undoubtedly and literally choked off lots of people of the more well-to-do classes. Time was when

[Continued on page 204.

one could ride along the high road practically dust-free—windy days excepted —but now one has to seek the by-road in the pious hope that there the automobile may cease from troubling and the dust be at rest. Not that this banishment has been without its compensations. As a result of seeking refuge from the car the cyclist has penetrated to many a sleepy hollow which would have gone unvisited had he stuck to the main routes, and has added vastly to his general knowledge of the country. In some districts the by-roads are as good as, if not better, than the high roads, on account of their freedom from heavy traffic. The hedges on either side are not spoilt by a cloak of dust; there are no telegraph posts to mar the scenery and remind one of the hustle which one wants to forget; and the very fact that the roads are comparatively narrow, and often as crooked as the branch of an old apple-tree, adds to their charm. That excellent series of books—guide-books, I cannot, in fairness to the authors, term them—about the by-ways and highways of several of our counties, will, if carefully read, add greatly to the zest of exploration among the hinterlands of stock routes.

※ ※ ※

Cycles and Luggage ONCE more organised revolt against the charges made by the railways for the carriage of cycles accompanied by their owners has reared its head, and is endeavouring to secure modifications. Of one thing we may be certain—that a very large section of the community would hail with delight a decision on the part of the companies to treat cycles as ordinary personal luggage, because in these days of huge congested cities the town cyclist is being increasingly penalised by the difficulty of shaking off the streets when he seeks country air. The prevalence of tram-lines is his special bugbear, not to say danger. Even where there are no tram-lines, the heavy traffic produces bumpy roads, in summer time converted into a series of puddles by the water-cart. To go one stage further, and assume a good, untrammed road, there yet remains the monotony of pedalling through miles of houses, which by itself is enough to discourage many a half-planned country spin.

To take you quickly into the heart of things there is the railway. Sixpence or less will land *you* half a dozen miles out among the trees and flowers. I underline the personal pronoun, because it is painfully true that the cycle will absorb another sixpence. There's the rub. Why should Jones be allowed to take his portmanteau, hat-box, and gun-case—as likely as not scaling together considerably more than the maximum "free" weight—for nothing, though Smith has to pay extra for his 30lb. machine, albeit his strictly personal luggage is confined to a pipe and a tobacco pouch, and the afternoon paper? Is it *fair?* A lot of people think not. Railway companies reply that the cycle is a bulky, clumsy thing, which gives their employés so much trouble and occupies so much room, that they'd rather not cultivate it. "Take it, if you must; but if you must, pay you must." Then comes the further question: What constitutes personal luggage? Round this the waves of argument rise higher year by year, as the cycle establishes more firmly its claim to be reckoned among the necessaries of everyday life. And surely what is a necessary is personal. Again, what *is* a necessary? Is a trunk full of extra clothes more indispensable than a cycle? It depends on circumstances and occasion.

The cyclist, on pleasure bent, regards his machine as absolutely necessary, and, rail or not, won't go without it. This brings us to another point. "Is it *expedient* for the railway companies to make a set at the poor cycle?" Which would pay them better, to squeeze the cyclist, or to encourage him? In the absence of definite facts and figures any conclusions as to the lucrativeness of their present attitude is impossible. Furthermore, even though a good solid sum be netted by the charges on the machine, who shall say how much has been lost in the fares, of folk who would pay for themselves but not for their machines? The cycle is treated with greater toleration abroad. A penny will frank a machine an indefinite distance in France. I have even registered four machines for that sum. At home everything is against the cycle; including double cloak-room charges, and refusal to accept liability for damages, unless an insurance fee be paid. From time to time concessions have been wrung from the reluctant companies; and it is not too much to hope that we may yet live to see the parliamentary ticket secure a place in the van for the cycle as well as a seat in a carriage for its owner. One doesn't like the idea of compelling the already, in many ways, harassed railroads by law. It would be vastly more gracious if they moved with the times, and voluntarily deferred to a widely spread public sentiment.

※ ※ ※

Tips My tame tipster has fired off several things at me lately. First, he recommends a fold or two of stout paper buttoned under the coat as an impromptu protection against evening cold. Having tested this idea he found the effects grateful and comforting. It should certainly justify itself, for have we not heard of the chilly railway passenger wrapping up his legs in the discarded daily when the woollen rug is far away? Not so long ago there was quite a boomlet in paper blankets for the poorer members of society. I haven't heard much of them lately. Possibly they crackled too much to encourage the approach of Morpheus. Anyway, when next you have to thread the darkling roads, and the air is too nippy to be pleasant, and you are at the wrong end of the journey to reach for your coat, try the paper dodge. It can't do any harm, and may stave off a chill.

The next wheeze is to be remembered when the cable of a Sturmey-Archer change-gear snaps, and you find yourself suddenly reduced to the lowest speed. The spindle has a slot in it near the step end to give you a view of an internal tell-tale sliding bar actuated by the cable. When the middle speed is "in," the end of this bar is, or should be, flush with the inside end of the slot; but it projects outwards a quarter of an inch or so when the lowest speed comes into operation. Therefore, should your cable part, pull the bar inwards and insert a wooden wedge into the slot, and you will be able to ride on the normal gear.

If a handle grip comes loose, don't try to stick it on with an adhesive which softens with heat, as many of them do; but try a compound called " Cæmentium." That will hold.

To attach a bulky or flat wide parcel to a narrow carrier so that it shall not slide about sideways, the straps should be given a turn round the edge bars of the carrier. As this prevents them slipping the parcel is held fast.

※ ※ ※

Be Ready in Time THE Easter holidays are already upon us, and some cyclists, no doubt, lament that they didn't order the new machine, or get certain repairs done to the old one a bit sooner. At this time of the year cycle manufacturers, agents, and repairers are "rushed" badly, because the public has delayed till the last moment, and then wants everything done in a hurry. If you have been bitten at Easter, learn the lesson before Whitsun. What is more exasperating than to discover on the eve of a holiday that "we can't undertake to deliver within a week," or that an undertaking made is accompanied by a think-yourself-lucky-if-you-get-it look in the eye. Neglected tyres consider it a point of honour to burst just an hour before the start for the two hundred mile run round. Chains and bearings show their teeth when you are well on the road, and as for ill-treated brakes, they, of course, fail in the middle of a steep hill. To the honour of cycles be it that they endure as much neglect as they do without breaking out. It used to be the fashion to cosset them and vex them with attentions that included unnecessary exploration of their vital parts. Now 'tis rather the reverse. The machine does its work, and is flung aside till it is wanted again, *sans* oil, *sans* cleaning, *sans* adjustment, *sans* anything but the right to prop itself up against the wall.

※ ※ ※

The New Bicycle THE possession of a new cycle has its anxieties as well as its pleasures. If you are a fatalist you let the machine take its chance when left where you can't keep an eye on it for a while—and the chances are greatly in favour of its being left alone; if prudent and cautious, you entwine it with a chain and padlock; but if of a nervous disposition, you are not even thus freed from fear of the gentlemen who traffic in other folks' belongings. Anxiety is relieved by insuring the machine with a good office, which can be done for a matter of five shillings or so. It must be very unpleasant in any case to find yourself minus the prized roadster, but 'twill ease the discomfort to remember that representations in the proper quarter will enable you to recover at least the major part of the money sunk in the errant wheel. The attractions of a brand new bike for the dishonest mind one can understand ; but it seems a trifle strange that some cycle-sneaks should be so undiscriminating as to risk their liberty for an old crock. Or is it that they think that the old 'un is less easily traced, whereas Sikes on a very smart turnout might arouse suspicion in the (often very shrewd) brain covered by the policeman's helmet ? Occasionally the thief is kind unawares. A friend of mine had a machine stolen which—in my opinion—was a potential death-trap, but which the friend in question would not pension off while it still held together somehow. Then, in a lucky hour, he left it at the kerb, outside a shop, and when he came out it had vanished. I should have liked to be present when the borrower tried to raise a little money on it at the cycle-hire shop. If he got a florin for it he did well. He stole better than he knew—for the owner.

Before leaving this section I would remind my readers that a number is generally stamped on the parts of a cycle. If this be duly noted the chances of recovering a stolen or strayed machine will be materially increased. Not long ago I saw the mention of the recovery of a cycle, which otherwise carried no distinguishing mark, through the police observing the number on the three-speed hub with which it was fitted.

* * *

Cycle Camping Again A CONTRIBUTOR to the official organ of the Association of Cycle Campers writes anent " Fixed Continental Camping," that " the chief difficulty was the finding of a camp site on which we should be permitted to stay for three weeks, and this necessitated a preliminary visit to the district selected. . . . Needless to say, it is essential that at least one of the party should have more than a smattering of the language of the country in which it is decided to camp." The difficulty mentioned was apparently confined to the neighbourhood of towns, as in the heart of the country " wonderment is expressed that one should think it necessary to ask permission to camp."

A Genuine Light-weight AMONG the most promising light motor-cycles now on the market is the Moto-Reve. The proof of the pudding is in the eating ; and as I haven't yet had an opportunity of trying this new-comer under petrol, I cannot talk of its paces. But if finish and design are guarantees of good behaviour on the road—and to a great extent they certainly are—then the Moto-Reve is all right. Its " insides " are on a diminutive scale. The fly-wheel weighs only 8lbs. or so ; the pistons are but 2ins. in diameter ; and other parts of the mechanism are in proportion. But the makers have avoided a serious defect that marred most of the early small motor engines by giving the fly-wheel spindles and bushes a generous length. I had almost forgotten to state that the engine is of the two-cylinder V-type, a type which has a very vibrationless action at all speeds, owing to the good balance obtained by setting the cylinders at an angle to one another.

Each cylinder has a small cock at the top for the injection of paraffin or petrol. This is a very good feature. In some cycles the release of a sticky piston is a troublesome business through lack of such fittings. The magneto, which weighs only 5lbs. or so, is driven through enclosed gearing. There is no chain to give trouble. All the pinions of the gear are marked so that they may be reassembled easily. Two of the pinions are mounted eccentrically, to produce a very quick rupture of the magneto's contact-breaker. Other points worthy of notice are the strong English-made frame and " Druid " spring-forks ; long handle-bars ; glass gauge on the petrol tank (capacity six pints) ; large inlet valves and direct drive by a V-section belt, claimed by the cognoscenti to give the greatest efficiency. The gear is 1 to 6, and the nominal horse-power 2 (on the brake considerably more), so the machine, which " all on " scales but a little over 8olbs., ought to be a good hill-climber. We may expect to see a considerable number of " Motor Dreams " about this summer.

* * *

Light v. Heavy Cycle IF you have hitherto used the heavy " full roadster " you might give the light-weight a trial next time you buy—not to replace the other, but as an addition to your stud. For different conditions, different machines. In sloppy weather the generously mud-guarded friend that has served you so well may be preferred. When shopping, you find its large carrier behind the saddle very useful. But when the roads are in first-class order, and the sun shines, and you want a good spin to clear out the cobwebs, then, I say, out with the little 25-pounder. Why pedal a superfluous half-stone or more? Don't be afraid of knocking the little one to pieces. Hasn't its kind taken record-breakers from Land's End to John o' Groats, over precious bumpy roads in places, and at a pace that you are not likely to keep up for long? After a while, whenever you intend to go out a-wheel, you will instinctively lead forth your feather-weight. Very possibly you will some day transfer the carrier, and take the new joy a-touring, and come back wondering how you ever endured that other.

For a short trip over level country 10lbs. may not much odds either way. But do a hundred mile — even fifty mile—ride, and the leg muscles will know all about the difference. Apart from actual riding the light-weight has the charm of being so easily lifted over a gate or stile—which one has to surmount now and then in one's roamings—or carried across the station footbridge when porters are not to be found, or hoisted in and out of the guard's van, or run up the front steps that lead to many a cyclist's home.

✣ ✣ ✣

The Dursley Pedersen AMONG light-weight cycles the Dursley Pedersen takes a leading place. Its most ardent admirers would not call its curiously triangulated frame beautiful, for the criss-cross of tubes has not the simple and satisfying outline of the "diamond"; but there is no getting over the fact that the D.P. is marvellously strong for its weight, being designed on thoroughly scientific lines. I don't think that, on the score of avoirdupois, anyone could reasonably cavil at a machine which, with three-speed hub, mudguards, brakes, wallet *and* tools, scales exactly 28¼lbs.; and as for strength, I have never heard of a D.P. finding its rider too much for it to bear. I am told that the company has practically discontinued the manufacture of two-speed gears, as every purchaser now asks for the three-speed hub. This last has been essentially improved of late by the substitution of a toothed clutch for the older type, which depended on friction for its gripping power. The friction clutch had a nasty knack of slipping, as its bigger brother of the motor-car does at times, and causing the rider to say, or at least think, things. The present clutch is as positive as one could wish it to be. This may partially account for the increasing popularity of the D.P. machine.

✣ ✣ ✣

Some Interesting Facts THE *Scientific American* number for February 22nd, 1908, records some very interesting experiments made by Professors Atwater and Rosa, of Wesleyan University, on the efficiency of the human body as a machine. The apparatus employed for measuring energy was a bicycle with its back wheel raised a little way from the ground so that its rim should revolve in air between magnets energised by a dynamo. The cycle was enclosed in a chamber artificially ventilated and heated. For hours together a cyclist pedalled the machine. His food and drink were carefully weighed, and the weight of the carbon contained in the air expired from his lungs was estimated by circulating the atmospheric contents of the chamber through chemical solutions. The moisture expired was also measured; while the other factor, the energy developed by the rider, was calculated in electrical units. The results showed that the rider actually delivered as work 21 per cent. of the energy contained in the food fuel supplied to him, which compares favourably with the 13 per cent. of fuel energy delivered by an up-to-date steam engine. Another 20 per cent. was expended on the internal animal mechanism of the rider. Professor Atwater concluded that under the first head alone the human machine is more efficient than any engine yet devised.

The competitors in a six-day cycle race were also made the subject of observation, their food (all carefully analysed that its fuel value should be known) being passed through the scales. "It is estimated," says our informant, "that the winner of this race, in the first twenty-four hours, did work that was equivalent to lifting twenty million pounds one foot, or, to state it otherwise, that was equal to lifting 3,825lbs. (nearly two tons) to a height of one mile. An ordinary labourer, doing average toil, develops in that length of time an amount of energy sufficient to raise two million pounds one foot. Whence it appears that this human machine, who led in the bicycle contest, delivered as much power as ten such labourers put together."

This is very interesting. So, also, is the professor's calculation that one-fourth of the total energy developed was expended in overcoming air-resistance. The winner, who covered 2,007 miles in the 144 hours, an average of fourteen miles an hour from start to finish, lost only 4lbs. in weight. "No other machine," concludes the article, "is nearly so economical [as the human body], or will continue in operation for so long a time without wearing out, with so small an expenditure for repairs. The human machine will outlast five of the most improved locomotives; it will keep in running order three times as long as a first-class printing press, and its 'life' is twelve times as long as that of the newest type of automobile. For a given amount of fuel, it yields twice the work of a locomotive engine. In short, it stands to-day unapproached by any energy-producing contrivance known."

So puny Man has still reason to take pride in the mortal frame which some folk compare so slightingly with those of other animals lower in the scale.

* * *

The Easy-Payments System THERE are signs that this system has seen its palmy days, so far as the cycling trade is concerned, though many firms still hold it out as an inducement to impecunious folk who cannot lay the cash on the counter in a lump sum. Of its success there can be no question. During the last eighteen months a huge number of cycles have been purchased " in bits." But there seems to be reason to think that most of the success has fallen to a section of the buying public, who, after paying a few instalments, have eluded the necessity for clearing their title to the machine in various ways— the simplest being to become insolvent. In many cases, though the full sum due has been extracted, the process has entailed so much trouble that serious doubts as to the game being worth the candle have disturbed the air of Coventry. An alternative to the easy-payment is the hire-purchase system, under which the vendor remains legal owner until the sum agreed upon has been paid over in full as hire by the prospective buyer. This also has had a considerable vogue, and from the vendor's point of view has its advantages, since it entitles him to seize the machine in default of payments, and so end the matter; whereas under the easy-payment scheme the machine belongs to the owner from the moment the first instalment is paid, and the vendor can sue for money only.

Personally, I am in sympathy with a writer in the *Cycle and Motor Trader*, who says: "I like neither [easy-payment or hire-purchase], for, as I have contended on other occasions when these subjects were under discussion, such systems are in the nature of inducements to people to incur liabilities which, generally speaking, they ought not to incur. The class of people who buy goods under such systems live from hand to mouth, and one week out of employment will frequently render them hopelessly insolvent."

A working man said to me recently, "It's no good preaching thrift to our young fellows, while there's this easy-payment system about." He was speaking of the system in general—for cycles are not the only things that attract youngsters —and his testimony, as coming from a member of the social class most affected, carries weight.

When a lad wants a thing he generally wants it mighty badly, and often throws prudence to the winds in order to gratify his wish. Then, as soon as he has possessed the coveted object a week or so, and the first flush of enjoyment has passed, and he sees a dismal string of payments ahead— well, he repents at leisure, but still he's got to work off a debt quite out of proportion to his means. Black care presently perches behind the saddle as he rides—assuming him to be of honest intentions.

The system is, of course, perfectly legitimate, and in many cases quite unobjectionable; yet to those who intend trying it I say—think it over very carefully first. It is bad business to buy a thing with money which you haven't got. Rather wait till you have the cash saved, and then hand it over. It is better for you, and it pleases the manufacturers, who show their appreciation by a substantial reduction in the price, as compared with the sum total of the instalments.

※ ※ ※

Roll Films   IN one respect the roll film is decidedly preferable to the thin cut film—the part exposed to the lens keeps flat owing to its being in a state of tension. Some cut films of which I have had experience buckled so badly that with a large stop there were areas imperfectly focused, even scratched by getting in the path of the shutter. This defect becomes more aggravated with an increase in the size of the film. So I prefer the roll for some purposes; and when I use separate films I like them *thick*. Roll films are very easily developed if one has the proper apparatus, which obviates the need for cutting them up before development, as was done in old times. American ingenuity has been largely responsible for the new mechanical devices which render a dark room less necessary than it was formerly. Films should be fresh, and developed as soon as possible after exposure. The celluloid support sets up chemical action of a kind that cannot occur in the case of glass plates; it is, therefore, the celluloid rather than the sensitive film that is the cause of deterioration.

※ ※ ※

A Copying Hint   THE "reflex" camera may be used for copying photographs, prints, or diagrams in the following manner: Screw a large board at right angles to the end of a table (one of the commoner sort, for obvious reasons), its lower part overlapping the edge a foot or so. The angle is tested with a square, and corrected by screwing the bottom of the board up towards a batten fastened to the nearer legs, or wedging it away, as the case may be. A line is drawn vertically down the centre of the board and continued along the top of the table, square to the board. Take a box, a foot long, eighteen inches wide, and six inches deep, and mark the ends vertically down the centre. These marks will act as guides in conjunction with the line on the table. On the top of the box draw two lines parallel to the centre and as far apart as the camera is wide. Place the camera on the box between the lines, and advance it up to the board, on which a horizontal line is drawn at the level of the centre of the lens. To complete the business additional cross and vertical lines should be made on the board to assist in making central of the thing to be copied.

Focusing becomes very simple work after these preliminaries, since the camera can be guided along the box, and the box along the table, perfectly square to the board. The advantages of the reflex also come to your aid. You can look down on the screen image, instead of having to crouch under a cloth, and the plate can be put in place and bared before focusing commences. As soon as the focus is satisfactory you release the mirror, an act which need cause no displacement of the image on the plate.

※ ※ ※

Cycle and Camera   WHEN you and the camera go out cycling the position of the camera will be regulated by its weight, or your own personal pet theories. If the thing be small, it is thrust into the outside pocket, and leaves a permanent mark of its sojourn. If somewhat bulky, it dangles from a strap hung round the body, or is perched on a rear carrier, or triced up inside the frame. Under several heads —those, for instance, of freedom from dust, and freedom from vibration—the back is the proper place for the camera, provided it be not of large size. It may be borne there without discomfort to the bearer if the strap be of a sufficient width to distribute the weight over the shoulder. The narrow, angular leather strap is an abomination. Far better is the brown webbing such as you see on a fisherman's creel. It may not be very sightly, but that doesn't matter. At the end of a long day the polished beauty of a decent black strap won't ease the galled shoulder. The strap should be long enough to allow the case to be pulled round easily when you want to fire a shot. Don't have the camera slung up in that part of the back which you can't reach to scratch. It is a good plan to change shoulders from time to time on a long day's riding. One advantage of carrying the camera on the back is that it is much more accessible than if strapped to the cycle; another, that you always have it with you if you part from your machine for a while to stroll about, and it therefore becomes more generally useful. The stand, if you carry one, must be attached to the frame or carrier, and in such a manner that it does not rattle. It's worth taking a good deal of trouble to fix up an arrangement which shall protect you from the clatter of a tripod. If possible, attach the case in such a position that the stand can be extracted without dismounting the case itself. This will save a considerable amount of time if you have to get the stand out frequently. About the worst position for a camera is the lamp-bracket, for there it will be invaded by dust thrown up by the wheel, unless the case be absolutely air-tight. Fine grit plays havoc with slides and shutters, to say nothing of covering the negatives with a multitude of pinholes.

* * *

Take Your Time THE film roll and various quick-change devices for plates have greatly extended the sphere of the photographer, and have also tempted him into slovenly habits. Now that the taking of a snap means merely the winding of a button and the release of a catch, too little attention is often given to the observations that should precede exposure. For instance, many a snap-shottist thinks little of the size of the important part of the image provided that it is visible on the finder. He does not duly consider whether the colours of the subject will be satisfactorily represented in monotones, and is disappointed to find what a slab sort of print he obtains. Again, he pays small heed to the relative positions of the various parts of the picture, and afterwards regrets that something is half hidden, or that some undesirable object has been included. Again, he takes his chance with the lighting, and discovers too late that the picture is without the relief afforded by a correct lighting angle. What is the total result ? He finds his album encumbered with a multitude of prints which possess little, if any, artistic merit, and begins to think that photography as a hobby is a bit over-rated.

But where time permits, let him exercise some self-restraint, and not make the exposure until he is satisfied that he has done his part towards making the forthcoming negative one that will be worth having. To amateurs of the over-hasty sort it would be a liberal education to accompany for a day or two an experienced worker with a ten-by-twelve outfit, who tries to make a swan out of a duck, and isn't content to let a duck represent a swan—who, in short, means to get all that is possible out of every prospect before which he pitches his camera. The snap-shot man is quite astray if he supposes that the canons which govern the time exposure are foreign to his branch of the art. On the contrary, the snap-shot is on all fours with the time-shot ; the length of exposure is a detail determined by circumstances. Given a fast enough lens, the specialist in interiors would be quite willing to reduce his exposures many times. It is what goes before the exposure, whether the subject be a cathedral or a steeple-chase, that tells. A snap-shot might be indistinguishable from a picture made with the aid of the cap, provided the conditions were the same for both. So don't cultivate the error that because a shutter is fast, you must hurry through your part of the business.

* * *

The Wide-open Eye IN what I may call gipsy photography a good eye half wins the battle by itself. Let me explain. A general was watching a battle, and someone pointed out to him how magnificently a regiment was charging down a slope. " Fudge," said he, " a haggis could charge *down* a hill ! " Similarly, anyone can impress an image on to a film, or rather get the light to do it, but it takes something more than mere mechanism to obtain anything worthy of the name of picture. The great thing is to be selective. Under some circumstances it's better to speak only when one has something worth saying ; and when you're out with a camera it's best to snap only when there's something worth snapping. And such a thing is not very far to seek if you possess the good eye. You meet a number of people bringing water from the village well. First comes a man, carrying the pails without effort, just as most men would. Let him pass. Next, a woman, with a hoop round her to prevent the pails coming too close. Here's something more suggestive. But keep your plate for the little chap behind, who is struggling along with but one pail, and every line in his body denoting a struggle. Now, here's effort. If your camera will only catch the posture in time, just the posture of the boy—that's the whole thing—then you've expended a film well. As your friend looks at the print he says, "That little chap's got all his work cut out for him." The mere comment shows that you have succeeded in conveying a distinct impression. The ideal album would contain nothing but prints which either suggest or teach.

※ ※ ※

Quick Printing   SOME amateurs are afraid of bromide paper because it requires care in the exposure and must be developed. Yet it has very distinct good features of its own. Given a good negative and correct timing, it yields delightfully soft artistic prints hardly to be distinguished from platinum prints; and as regards speed of work it beats P.O.P., with all its wearisome examination of frames, out of the field. If you have a number of negatives to print off, first classify them with regard to density, and work through them batch by batch, using the same exposure for all of a batch, as soon as the correct time has been found with a test strip, and developing them off the reel. It is a vast mistake to jump from thick negative to thin, and back to thick. You never know where you are. Bromides score heavily in that they can be printed at night by artificial light, some of the slower kinds not even requiring non-actinic light for development. The Kodak Company's "Dekko" papers come under this heading, and are much appreciated by workers who have used them. The "velvet" surface paper is the one I prefer for all-round purposes. It is a compromise between "glossy" and "matte," and as such possesses some of the merits of both. It gives detail without flatness. For reproductions by the half-tone block process the glossy is the thing, however.

※ ※ ※

Classifying Information   MOST photographers take in one or more photographic journals. One week there is nothing of particular interest, so you throw your journal aside and stack it with its predecessors, which have already grown distressingly numerous and dusty. Next week you strike an edifying paragraph or article, read it carefully, and pigeonhole some of the information in your mind. That number presently goes to swell the heap, and a month later you want to refer back to the matter that arrested your attention. Then commences a wearisome hunt, unless you have been careful to make a note on the cover. You could save yourself a lot of trouble by cutting out all interesting stuff at once and filing it away in long envelopes opening along the top—not at the end—each having the subject written large at the left upper corner. These envelopes are filed away in alphabetical order, in a drawer or tray of suitable dimensions. The further the subdivision of headings is carried the more easily is anything found. A collection of this kind becomes extremely valuable, much more so than the average text-book designed on the stereotyped lines, as you lay under contribution the experiences and wisdom of a thousand workers.

※ ※ ※

Forthcoming Dress Styles   I GATHER that the forthcoming season will bring practically no changes in men's fashions. "There are comparatively few departments," says *Men's Wear*, "in which the novelty element is at all conspicuous. Perhaps at this stage in the history of the men's wear trade it is becoming increasingly difficult to evolve anything which proclaims itself as absolutely new; and, in addition, the difficult times are against experiment of the more venturous sort. It is not, however, intended to provide the impression that the wholesale houses have abandoned the idea of aggressive enterprise, but rather that they have been content to proceed this season on somewhat conservative lines, in the apparent hope that a more profitable result will attend their operations.

"Turning to the matter of styles the single-breasted reefer jacket again possesses no serious rival. In most cases the cut has been slightly modified, the length of the garment having been curtailed, and the roll carried a trifle further up the coat. It is still, however, made with a noticeable amount of 'waist,' and with the long-favoured back slit. The popularity of this type of suit is so firmly established that whatever may happen to the roll and other characteristic details in the West End tailoring trade, little prospect of its fall from high estate in the fashions of the million need be contemplated for a long time to come.

"In coloured tweeds the shades of

THE SPORTSMAN'S VIEW POINT

green and brown are again prominent, some of the hues enthusiastically praised in the warehouses being somewhat too extreme to be designated really artistic. The inevitable greys are as strongly represented as ever, and, this said, little further need be mentioned relative to the colour question.

"The imitation home-spun, which has been brought to such a state of perfection that certain of the cloths might well deceive expert eyes, will undoubtedly play a most important part in the coming season, and here again the strongly marked brigade are receiving the greater attention."

❋ ❋ ❋

Burberry Ideas — *Men's Wear* notwithstanding, I shall be very much surprised if the enterprising firm of Burberry, Limited, do not introduce, as usual, some of their up-to-date ideas for the sporting man. No house I know of works with such an exceedingly intimate knowledge of what a sportsman really requires as Messrs. Burberry, and, personally, whether I am requiring new clothes or not, I can always amuse myself for an odd half-hour or so by looking through the list of this firm, and noting how remarkably ingenious their designers seem to be in adapting tailoring methods to the requirements of sportsmen.

❋ ❋ ❋

Fishing Men's Gear — IN a somewhat narrower field the same may be said of Messrs. Anderson, Anderson & Co., the well-known fishing waterproofs manufacturers of Queen Victoria Street, E.C. Indeed, I am very much inclined to doubt whether there exists in the world a firm which caters more aptly for fishing men's waterproofs—rubber boots, rubber stockings, waders, brogues, etc.—than Messrs. Anderson. I had occasion to use a pair of their waders a week ago, and on turning them out for this season's trout-fishing I was astonished to find how extraordinarily well these waders had kept. All of which, I imagine, goes to show that for really good and useful sporting clothes one *must* go to those tailors who make a speciality of sporting clothes, and whose cutters cut from the point of view of the sportsman, and *not* from that of the average tailor.

The Riding Breeches Builder — THERE is, for instance, no form of sporting garment that is more difficult to get well cut and properly fitting than a pair of riding breeches, and yet there is not a tailor in London—or, for that matter, on the face of the civilised globe—who will not cheerfully take an order for a pair of riding breeches, and with sanguine *abandon* guarantee a perfect fit, although his riding breeches orders may amount to no more than two per annum.

❋ ❋ ❋

The Becoming Limit — SOME time ago a rather amusing quotation caught my eye. It was as follows:—

"*I dare do all that may become a tailor, who dare do more is none.*"

This ingenious parody emanated from Messrs. William Evans & Co., of Great Portland Street, W. A little later I recommended a friend to this firm in the matter of some riding breeches, and he has since informed me that the company have turned him out a really excellent pair. Those who are dissatisfied with their present tailor cannot do better than call on Messrs. Evans.

❋ ❋ ❋

Bantry Tweeds — I NOTE that Mr. R. B. Marston, the popular editor of the *Fishing Gazette*, has been extolling the Bantry "home-spun" tweeds, and I can agree with him that for angling, shooting, and golf suits these Irish tweeds are enormously serviceable. Mr. Thomas Copithorne, of Bantry, Ireland, from whom free patterns may be obtained, has found a process by which these tweeds are waterproofed, and, further, entirely obviates the possibility of their shrinking. They are made in a variety of shades. There is an old shooting-coat of mine which bears silent witness as to the hard-wearing capacity of these tweeds every time I put it on.

❋ ❋ ❋

The Silk Hat and Cigarettes — ALTHOUGH I have not consulted any high authorities, nor burrowed in statistics, it occurs to me that the silk hat is disappearing at no uncertain rate. Certainly, ten years ago, one, walking down the Strand, would have encountered twice as many silk hats as he does now. At least, that is how it struck me the other day.

I may, of course, have chosen a "slack" hour for silk hats; but it seems to me that the decreasing numbers of those who wear "toppers" provides a more feasible explanation. Incidentally, I noticed more men smoking cigarettes than I have ever noticed before; and, thirdly, I observed that the majority of those who smoked did not wear glasses, and most of those who wore glasses were not smoking. As I have already said, I may have struck an unusual hour; but I think that those who will walk down this thoroughfare, and amuse themselves by taking note of the things I have mentioned, will come to very much the same conclusion.

* * *

Safety Razors FEW articles appertaining to the toilet have taken such a complete hold upon the affections of men generally in recent years as the safety razor. Many men I have met cling tenaciously to the old style, and, indeed, there is no overwhelming reason why they should not. After a certain age a man is loth to slough an old familiar custom; but on the whole I imagine that the safety razor is going to be the razor of the future. Certainly, if all safety razors are of as good a quality as those of Messrs. Seabrook Brothers, of Featherstone Street, E.C., this quality constitutes a very strong argument in favour of the modern safety razor.

* * *

An Esquimaux Dress Fashion READING some books on the Arctic recently I came across some interesting facts in the matter of dress—or rather the lack of it—which may interest readers of these notes. From one of these books—Nansen's "First Crossing of Greenland," I believe it was—I learnt that it is the custom of the Esquimau, on leaving the bitter open air for the equally bitter (to civilised senses) though undoubtedly warmer, air of his snow hut, to shed every stitch of clothes that he wears. For immemorial years the Greenlanders have followed this custom; but when the missionaries gradually found their way to their bleak, inhospitable shores, they, being righteously shocked, induced the Esquimaux with bribes or threats, or both, or possibly neither, to adopt an indoor dress, which one might easily assume consisted of more or less civilised garments, selected or suggested by the missionaries. Almost simultaneously with the introduction of this indoor-clothes custom for the Esquimaux came consumption — a disease hitherto unknown among these inhabitants of the cold regions, and they died off like flies. There is a moral behind all this somewhere, the obvious moral, of course, being "Don't wear clothes in the Arctic," but, as Mark Twain might put it, I have an instinct which tells me that there is something wrong with the obvious moral. Seriously, I do not pretend to explain this most interesting fact.

* * *

The River Costume IT is a far cry from Greenland to Twickenham, but it occurs to me for thorough comfort and grace of appearance there is no more perfect dress in the whole world than the dress of the average boating man. The light, soft flannel, the light and easy footgear, the airy blazer, and the comfortable Panama, all go to produce "a consummation most devoutly to be wished," or words to that effect; at any rate, the boating costume is one which will never lack wearers.

A Week-End on a Motor-Cycle

FROM A BEGINNER'S POINT OF VIEW

By BERNARD PARSONS

IT was Dunn who, having taught me to ride, purchase, and enjoy a motor-cycle, suggested a week-end trip in company in order that I should experience the last delight but one of motor-cycling. The last, of course, is motor-cycle camping—but opportunity for that was lacking.

The trip that he mapped out was to lovely Buxton *via* Chesterfield and home over the hills through the beautiful Derbyshire dales by way of Nottingham, and so on by the great North Road through Melton Mowbray, famous for its pork-pies; Oakham, renowned for nothing in particular; Uppingham, where so many great cricketers have spent their public school-days; and thence back to town by way of Kettering and Bedford.

We left London at 11.30 on the Saturday morning, and picking our way carefully through the crowded mid-day Saturday traffic of the Edgware Road and thence by the tram-lines which lead to Barnet, we puffed lazily along until we soon left the crowded streets of London behind. There are intrepid motor-cyclists who profess to show a superior disregard for traffic, and, in consequence, dash at top-speed boldly here and there whizzing past motor-omnibuses, gliding in between trams and other vehicles, and altogether taking risks which are quite unnecessary.

"Never travel fast in traffic," said Dunn, who, by the bye, for his enterprise in taking up fresh hobbies, was known among his friends as "the wise man not afraid to experiment," as we passed the "Red Lion" at Barnet, "for that's where many motor-cyclists are apt to come to grief. There are enough quiet country roads and to spare, and—here we have them," he concluded, as we turned into the road leading to St. Albans, whereupon he advanced his petrol lever, gave his machine a little more air, and shot gaily ahead.

I followed his example, and for the next ten miles or so we "pip-pipped" merrily away until we slowed up to smile benignly on a local wit who, with the air of one giving forth to the world an item of vastly important fact, imparted the news that our back wheels were going round. As a matter of fact, I don't think we should have wasted those smiles on the bucolic humorist had not a motor-car, coming in the opposite direction, informed us there was a police trap a short distance ahead. Police traps are not to be trifled with, so for the next mile or so we slowed down to an easy twelve miles an hour.

Soon the spire of St. Albans Cathedral rose towering above the skyline, seeming to keep watch over the pretty market town below, and as by this time it was

A Week-End on a Motor-Cycle

close on two o'clock, we decided to stop here for a light lunch before pushing ahead to Market Harborough, where we had arranged to spend the night—in fact, my friend, scorning to reply to my timorous hint that possibly we might never reach there at all, had wired on ahead to order a little *recherché* dinner for two, comprising some cold salmon and cucumber, a Surrey fowl, green peas, chip potatoes, asparagus, and stewed fruit and cream.

" You'll have the requisite appetite by the time you reach there," he said. Ruminating comfortably on the *menu* in store, I silently hoped he was right.

Shortly after three o'clock, having done perfect justice to the fare provided at the best hostelry in the place—motorcycling, somehow or other, puts a very keen edge on to one's appetite—and after trying to subdue into silence a garrulous waiter who would insist upon telling us that " St. Albans was a wonderful busy place, what with its trade for making hats and boots and ropes, and its printing works and its brewing and malting—wonderful fine breweries, they are here, thank heaven, gentlemen," he said with an animation doubtless stimulated by frequent indulgence in the brew he was advertising so enthusiastically, we put our bicycles on the stand to warm up the engines, got into alpaca once more, and ere the Cathedral clock chimed the quarter after three we were turning off on to the old coaching road leading to Dunstable, the next town of importance for which we were making.

The country was looking simply superb; the air was not too cold and not too hot —a " just right " day for a long ride, in fact—and now and again on a long open stretch of road we pushed our " advance " levers " all out," mentally praying that there might be a beautiful absence of police traps in the neighbourhood. And so it turned out, for although on my stop-watch I calculated that, by the milestones, we had done eight miles in just over eleven minutes, no gentlemen in blue sprang out from beneath the friendly shade of a dry ditch, or suddenly leapt into view from behind a sleepy-looking hay-rick, to inform us " that we had been travelling at over forty miles an hour, riding to the public danger," and so on, and so forth.

All this time I was wondering where those accidents and breakdowns said to be peculiar to motor-bicycles I had heard so much about had concealed themselves. And I continued to wonder in vain until, just after passing through Stoney Stratford we pulled up to mend a slight puncture in my back wheel. Ten minutes later we were both jogging merrily ahead again, and after slowing down to a comfortable eight miles an hour through Northampton, where, by the way, we stopped five minutes for a fill of petrol, we finally reached Market Harborough a few minutes before seven, having covered the distance of just over eighty miles at an average of about twenty an hour, as several times we had stopped on the way to enjoy a cigarette.

My friend was right. By seven o'clock we both had appetites of which the mightiest hunter need not have been ashamed, and we lingered over dinner with a staying power worthy of Lucullus.

A stroll round the town, a whisky and soda in the snug parlour of the hotel, where we listened for half an hour or so to the local bloods competing against each other over their past doughty deeds in a manner reminiscent of Ananias at the top of his form, brought the evening to a close.

One had the impudence to announce to the expectant company that he had once brought off a quadruple event which had netted him over four thousand pounds, which, however, he lost within a month ; another, a fisherman, told ferocious and wonderful yarns of mighty catches of salmon on the Norfolk Broads ! and a third, towards the close of the evening, had three quiet rounds with a friend of the name of Johnson to prove that he wasn't as good as " Tommy " Burns. Market Harborough is, indeed, a cheery spot—towards closing-time.

However, at 10.30 we gave the company a safety miss, and half an hour later Dunn and I were sleeping the sleep of all just motor-cyclists who have not exceeded the speed limit — more than they can help.

All good citizens in Market Harborough were still abed the next morning when, fortified by two glasses of milk—I had a dash of rum in mine, but I didn't tell my friend, because, after all, it was my own business—and a plateful of unpleasantly dry biscuits, a few minutes after five we set out for a long five-hours' early morning

A Week-End on a Motor-Cycle

ride by way of Chesterfield on to Buxton. Nothing untoward occurred to our machines, though once or twice we stopped on the way to allow our engines to cool—in the early morning you can push ahead at a rare speed with little fear of getting nailed by a police trap, or of annoying other users of the road.

We reached the old town of Chesterfield, with its Cathedral with that funny crooked steeple, which looks as if, every minute, it would topple over for good and all, shortly after eight, and while breakfast was being prepared we explored the town for a barber. Eventually we succeeded in getting a shave apiece at the shop of a worthy gentleman who endeavoured to attract the notice of customers by setting forth in a prominent place in his window the alluring and extravagant announcement that "each customer was provided with clean water."

Breakfast over—by the way, I can thoroughly recommend the Chesterfield bacon and eggs—we forged along once more at a good speed and reached Buxton at ten minutes past ten, rather dusty, to be sure, but otherwise thoroughly fit and well, and feeling on the best of terms with the world, ourselves, and our machines. There's nothing, believe me, like a good dose of early-morning air to make you feel that this old world of ours isn't really such a bad place after all.

The charms of Buxton and the neighbouring districts are too well known to call for further reference here. Let it suffice, therefore, that, after indulging in a second morning pipe at the world-famous "Cat and Fiddle," we filled up with petrol once more, and, just as church-going Buxtonians were wending their way to service, we turned our machines in the direction of home. After leaving Nottingham we struck the great North Road once more, and so on to Melton Mowbray, Oakham, and Uppingham, where we lunched at "The Falcon" at 2.30.

I should have liked to have visited the familiar scenes of days gone by, but time pressed; and though we did squeeze in a few minutes to visit the Upper Cricket

We filled up with petrol once more.

Ground, look in at the new school gymnasium, and call on one or two old friends, by four o'clock we were passing through Rockingham—the Rockingham Hill is a brute—on to Market Harborough, and thence to Kettering, where we had a scratch meal shortly after six.

A ten minutes' "pull-up" at Bedford for another fill of petrol, in case of accidents, was our last serious stop before lighting up a few miles outside Luton, where the countless hands employed at the straw manufactories there, while enjoying a Sunday evening stroll, took such a personal interest in us that one adventurous lass endeavoured to snatch my carrier as a keepsake.

At Barnet we pulled up for ten minutes for a smoke and a chat, and it was just ten-thirty when we reached home for supper, having covered well over 330 miles in a day and a half.

"Must just run my eye over the machine before I wash and change," I said with the air of a connoisseur as I—quite affectionately, I admit—jacked up the back wheel on the sturdy stand provided for the purpose, and proceeded to put my little knowledge about putting motor-bicycles " to bed " to the test.

"A fortnight ago you said that you thought all motor-bicycles and their riders ought to be consigned to the South of France, or somewhere even warmer than that," said Dunn, irrelevantly, as he watched me looking after my machine with the same sort of affection that a man shows for a good hunter that has carried him well in a long run.

I made no reply. But all the same I mentally blessed my friend " wise enough to experiment," for having introduced me to a really enjoyable, healthy, and inexpensive pastime, thinking the while what a lot of fun all and sundry miss who believe, to-day, the " scare " stories told about the many defects and drawbacks of the motor-cycle. Some years ago, perhaps, these stories may have been true. To-day they are terminological inexactitudes of the worst order.

But you may take it from me—and since describing this, my first long week-end ride, I have covered over four thousand miles on the same machine with but very few breakdowns and accidents—the motor-bicycle of to-day is thoroughly reliable—if only you treat it with the same consideration you would a horse or a motor-car. Neglect it, and you will inevitably have cause to abuse it. Look after it properly, treat it like a " pal," and—well, it will treat you likewise. There is a most faithful sense of reciprocity about the motor-bicycle

Light-Weight Motor-Cycles

By W. G. McMINNIES

(*Continued from article commencing in "Fry's Magazine" for July.*)

This is partly due to the excellent design of spring forks fitted on one or two of the most promising light-weights, and partly due to the general position of the rider. The position of the foot-rests on several machines makes a most natural riding position possible. The chain-stays are carried forward and divided into a T piece, whose arms are covered with rubber, and thus much of the vibration is eliminated. There is hardly any engine vibration when running fast, and still less when running slowly. In the case of a big single-cylinder machine quite the reverse is the case, for when the machine slows down below ten miles per hour the ominous plunking sets up, which gives the outsider the mistaken idea that all motor-cyclists suffer tremendously from the so-called vibration bugbear. Of course on modern machines this is non-existent.

On one machine which was tested the writer was greatly surprised to find that in addition to having a comfortable riding position it was also possible to use the pedals without undue contortions when assisting the little engine on hills. This was the first machine he had ever ridden where the happy combination of a comfortable pedalling and riding position had been found. Perhaps it might have been that this particular position just happened to suit his build, but it is a fact that on other machines, which may be comfortable enough when ridden on the foot-rests, the very reverse is the case on the few occasions when pedalling may be necessary. In fact, it is impossible to pedal at all unless one gets off the saddle and stands upon the pedals. Another point where the light-weight machine is seen to advantage over the heavier types is as regards its tyres. Most light-weights are fitted with 2in. tyres, and consequently are far more over-tyred in comparison to their power and speed than any other type. Many 4 and 5 horse-power machines capable of a speed of a mile a minute are fitted with no heavier tyres. So the owner of a light-weight need not be frightened of his tyre bill if he sees he gets a good pair of 2in. covers fitted to start with. These ought to last him almost for a whole season's riding; as, what with low speed, light weight, and an even beating twin engine, there should be very little wear indeed.

Several other points are just worth mentioning; the first is the question of brakes. The front brake will be found quite powerful enough to pull up any light motor-cycle, and it is possible to apply it very gradually. The back brake can be kept in reserve for emergencies. The use of the front brake should be cultivated on greasy roads, as it has been the writer's experience that it tends to skid the machine far less than if the back brake were suddenly applied. Belts will be found to act satisfactorily if kept in good condition. They are subject to a great strain on most light-weights owing to the small size of the engine pulley. This is, of course, necessary, as otherwise a sufficiently low gear would not be available. It has been found that a gear of $5\frac{1}{2}$ or 6 to 1 is best for these machines. So if a 24in. back drum is fitted this would only allow a 4in. pulley on the engine-shaft. Several makers have overcome the difficulty of slipping belts by internally gearing down the engine pulley. So that even with a 6 to 1 gear the engine pulley may be 6ins. or 8ins. in diameter. This method might be followed with advantage by other manufacturers. The writer sees no reason why some form of shaft-drive should not be employed on the twin-cylinder light-weights, which run so smoothly that there should not be any undue strain on the gear. The one disadvantage of a gear drive is that, when a breakdown has occurred, and it is necessary to get the machine home, it is impossible to disconnect the engine, but one has to push the machine and engine together. Of course, if a clutch is fitted it is different, but with a belt one simply removes it and pedals home. It is also quite easy to pedal the light-weight home in the case of a breakdown, as the only alteration needed is the raising of the saddle. On the whole the writer found the leather belt most satisfactory, especially when made on a scientific principle to gain maximum flexibility, which is what is needed most of all when a small pulley is used. It is not as clean to handle as a rubber belt, and it has to be frequently oiled and scraped, but it is not so liable to pull through at the fastenings, and does not slip when wet as much as a rubber one. If only the light-weight were fitted with a light form of two-speed gear it would be an ideal machine. An adaptation of the push-bicycle speed gear might be invented, when the steepest hills would have no terror for the man so mounted. At present makers are rather apt to sacrifice equipment to lightness. The luggage-carriers are not large enough to be worth the name, and the stands provided are inclined to be flimsy. But taking the light-weight all round the writer found it an ideal machine for handling in traffic and where the roads were bad. It was very comfortable, and quite reliable. He would infinitely prefer to ride this type of machine in winter, but would rather have a fast twin or single for doing long cross-country journeys in the summer when the roads are dry and fast travelling is possible. The light-weight in winter is open to improvement in one way. Owing to the position of the foot-rests on most of these machines the rider is apt to be bespattered with mud, snow, or whatever else happens to be on the road. This should be prevented by the fitting of an efficient mudguard. The writer rigged up an old pair of fisherman's waders to act as such, and very efficient they were. They were suspended from the handle-grips by the legs, and the waist part of the trousers hung down in front of the foot-rests and fully protected the rider's extremities. This was a great improvement in more ways than one, as the rest of the machine was kept quite clean, and it was much warmer for the rider, who got all the advantage of the heat of the engine. In time of war the light-weight should come in useful for reconnoitring roads, and it could also be ridden across country. Hedges and ditches would present no difficulties, for it could be lifted over such obstacles by two men with ease. Altogether the writer is convinced that, for men on the wrong side of forty, or for professional men who intend taking up motor-cycling, there is nothing like the light-weight.

One of the last machines to pass through the writer's hands was a $1\frac{1}{4}$ horse-power single-cylinder light-weight, which was tested over three hundred miles of hilly country. The makers claim that this machine only weighs 8olbs., and is capable of a speed of thirty miles an hour. This is quite true, as an average speed of twenty miles an hour was maintained for long distances across country. This machine was driven by a round leather belt, the correct tension of which was maintained by a jockey pulley. In use the belt was satisfactory, but the fastening gave trouble. The makers sent down half a dozen spare fasteners with the machine, but these were all used up after three hundred miles running. The jockey pulley was very useful for slacking off the belt after a day's ride, and saved one the dirty job of taking it off altogether.

Returning home late one night the machine ran out of petrol, but when filled up with paraffin—which luckily one could get near at hand—continued its way as merrily as ever. Indeed it seemed to run even better, but with a disagreeable smell from the exhaust. A good deal of pedalling was necessary on steep hills, and the pedalling gear was too low to materially aid the engine. This particular machine was fitted with shields on each side of the engine to ensure efficient cooling of the cylinder. These shields certainly help to protect the mechanism, and also the rider's clothes, from the oil and grease which unfortunately always seem to be present on a motor-cycle engine. Rather a neat fitment on this machine was a paraffin pump for injecting paraffin in the morning and freeing the piston.

Another good point was the position of the magneto, which was driven off the fly-wheel, and placed high up behind the cylinder. It is also protected by the aforementioned wind-shields, and is absolutely out of the way of all rain and mud;

which is more than can be said of the magnetos of even some of the best machines.

There is no doubt that the public are at last beginning to seriously consider the light-weight machine, and have become dissatisfied with the heavy twins and singles, which generally require such laborious starting. One of the leading light-weight manufacturers is already six weeks behind deliveries with his machines, and several others have almost more business than they can cope with. One of the chief hindrances to the coming of the light-weight is the growing adoption of free engine and two-speed gear devices on the heavier models, which make it possible to start these machines by hand and drive them off from a standstill on any hill. With the addition of a small two-speed gear and clutch the light-weight motor-cycle would indeed be an ideal machine. For a machine weighing 90lbs., and developing 2 to 3 horse-power gear, ratios of $4\frac{1}{2}$-1 and 9-1 would be very suitable. At present most light-weights are geared about $5\frac{1}{2}$ or 6 to 1.

In the recent article on "Passenger Motor-Cycles" no mention was made of the Lowen, a very excellent side-car which has two wheels running in track alongside the-motor-cycle. The rear wheel carries most of the weight, whilst the front one is coupled to the steering head of the machine, which is thus converted into a light motor-car. The makers claim that this is by far the safest type of side-car, for either right or left-hand corners can be negotiated at a good speed. It is also capable of being driven without a passenger. Another claim put forward on behalf of this side-car is that it strains the motor-cycle frame less than other single-wheel types. This would appear quite likely. This type of passenger machine can, like several others, be attached to and detached from the motor-cycle without difficulty in a few moments without the use of a tool. This is a point well worth studying by those who keep their machines indoors, or in places where little room is available.

The "Lowen" side-car in use.

The Motor-Cycle of To-day

By W. G. McMINNIES

FEW people seem to realise what a marvellous little special train they can get nowadays for between £40 and £50. The modern motor-cycle in many cases, especially across country, is capable of beating the train. It can travel distances of two hundred miles and more in a day, and only needs to be refilled with petrol. It is capable of all its big brother the car can do in the way of hill-climbing and speed, and is, in the hands of a man of average intelligence, equally reliable. There are at present on the market three classes of machines —the heavy-weight multi-cylinder, the medium-weight single-cylinder, and the light-weight. The medium-weight single-cylinder seems to be at present the most popular type, though the tendency is towards lightness and lower engine power, so that in the future we may see the two latter classes combine. To the ordinary man in the street the motor-cycle may seem a noisy, dirty, and uncomfortable conveyance. This may be the case with some, but certainly not with all, especially the latest models. Some of these are quite as silent as is desirable, for an absolutely silent machine would be a danger to the public and to its rider. The bugbear of vibration can easily be done away with by anyone. He has only to get on a machine and ride it, and he will find vibration practically non-existent, except over the worst roads, and then only at high speed. Even an ordinary bicycle would jolt under similar conditions. The modern machine is so reliable that it is not necessary for its rider to be always in a mess through having to make impromptu roadside adjustments. Indeed, the writer has recently heard of two intrepid motor-cyclists who rode thirty miles in dress clothes to a dinner party, and were none the worse, though, of course, they wore overalls.

The motor-cycle has not reached finality by any means, any more than has the motor-car. The following seem to be some of the more important improvements which will be found in the best and most useful machines. It is one of the most enjoyable things in the world to ride a fast machine along a dry road, but the reverse is the case if the road be hilly and greasy. The likelihood of a machine to skid on greasy roads has, without doubt, prevented many people from going in for one. The tyre makers have come forward with non-skid tyres to remedy this, and they have very nearly succeeded. But a fault they cannot cure is the inability of most present-day machines to climb steep hills at walking pace. Any good motor-cycle can roar up a dry hill at forty miles an hour, but when the road is muddy, and there is a hairpin corner, this is impossible. The remedy is a two-speed gear. Several leading makers have recognised this, and are placing two-speed machines on the market, the advantages of which are obvious. The ability to start from a standstill on any hill, to go as slowly as possible through congested traffic, and yet to have the power for fast travelling when required, will attract many new followers. Elderly men, too, have been prevented from getting a machine from seeing young fellows vault on to a machine when travelling twelve miles an hour; they also dislike the laborious pushing which is often necessary before the engine will start. The second point where improvement is needed is in the mud-guarding arrangements. Most machines are a disgusting sight after a hundred miles on a really dirty road; and, alas! this often applies also to their riders. The belt often throws up a lot of mud, and the front wheel is in many cases not as well protected as it should be. There is a screen at present on the market which, the makers claim, effectually shields its rider from all mud-splashes. It begins in front of the engine and continues over the belt. With the use of this one may go out on any day without overalls, and have no fear of returning covered with mud. When these two fitments, viz., the change-speed gear and effective mud-guarding, become standard there is no reason why everyone who can afford it should not have a machine. From the foregoing

The Efficiency of Light-Weight Motor-Cycles.

It is certainly a truism to state that the perfect motor-cycle is one that, whilst proving efficient in regard to every mechanical and engineering detail, shall also be light in weight.

There has until recently been a tendency to sacrifice weight to the question of speed, strength, and reliability, but with a perfect knowledge of the most successful of motor-cycles this has proved to be erroneous. To the proprietors of the "Motosacoche" we owe this enlightenment.

They have succeeded in producing a machine that whilst answering standard tests in regard to non-stop runs, hill-climbing, speed, reliability, is yet quite the lightest motor-cycle now on the market.

The Motosacoche attachment, manufactured under the patents of H. & A. Dufaux, is attachable to any make of cycle, and weighs but 35lbs., a fact that will surprise many who know the clumsy mechanism of the ordinary motor-bicycle. The Motosacoche attachment and latest model machine, as delivered by the company ready for use, weighs but 75lbs. complete.

The simplicity of the mechanism, the ease of control, and the general high class of the mechanical structure, will appeal to the discriminating. It is impossible here to go into details of the mechanism, but it may be said that the endeavour to overcome all the defects of old types has been successful. The following is the brief specification of the Magneto model (rigid frame):

Engine—Carburettor Dufaux patent. Economy—130 miles to the gallon of petrol. Ignition—magneto. Silencer—most efficient, and easily cleaned. Lubrication—splash. Cooling—shields direct a good current of air where it is wanted; over-heating unknown. Control—entirely from handle-bar. Cycle—built by the Rover Company, Ltd., Coventry. Frame—22in. standard. Wheels—26in. Tyres—1¾in. Clincher A1 light motor-cycle. Brakes—two powerful rim. Saddle—Lycett's special motor. Speeds—five to thirty miles per hour, and gradients of 1 in 10 mounted without pedal assistance.

The Magneto model (rigid frame, specially low built), details of which are given above, is a great favourite with the public, Dufaux's having sold a great number during last year. The price is low, being fixed for the British Isles at £33.

The Accumulator model is an equally efficient motor-cycle, manufactured by Dufaux's with the special type of ignition indicated by the name.

The Motosacoche is thus described by a trade expert: "I believe this, from the point of view of power, economy, and weight, is the most efficient motor-cycle which has been manufactured."

Any reader of FRY'S MAGAZINE who is interested should certainly write to the Company for a copy of their descriptive booklet. It will be sent post free on receipt of name and address. The various types of Motosacoche may be seen at the premises of Messrs. H. & A. Dufaux (England), Ltd., 65, Holborn Viaduct, London, E.C., who will at all times be pleased to explain the working parts, and to point out the reasons why the Motosacoche proves superior to any other form of motor-cycle. They will also be pleased to show a list of testimonials received from purchasers.

All applications for particulars should be sent to the address given.

The Ideal BREECHES for all Sportsmen

The "R.H." Puttee Breeches embody a simple idea (patented) that makes them both the most comfortable and the best finished breeches made. The puttee bands (shown in the illustration here) are *a continuation of the breeches*, made to wind round twice. No pinching laces or buttons are required; they fit the knee and fasten automatically. All who wear them declare the ease and comfort delightful.

The "R.H." Puttee Breeches.
PATENTED.

For Riding, Walking, Shooting, Golfing, etc.

Price from **24/-** complete.

Illustrated booklet, patterns, and self-measurement forms sent on application.

J. & G. ROSS,
32, Old Bond St., LONDON, W.; & EXETER.

Telephone: London, No 1312 Mayfair; Exeter, No. 46.

remarks it must not be thought that the present-day motor-cycle is inefficient; it is very far from that, and these are only two small points which might be improved.

The writer regards a fast motor-cycle as one of the most sporting things in the world. One cannot compare it with a motor-car, for there is just the difference between riding and driving. As most people are aware, many events have been organised to test the speed and reliability of present-day machines. Amongst these are hill-climbing competitions and speed tests, both on road and track. Some say there is nothing like tobogganing in Switzerland. Those who have competed for the Cresta Cup must have a thrilling time, tearing *down* hill and round corners at over fifty miles an hour. But just imagine the reverse. At a big hill climb, where perhaps there are one hundred competitors, some of the fastest machines ascend the hill at forty-five miles an hour. They tear round acute bends, which it requires all the skill of their riders to safely negotiate. One has only got to get astride a fast machine on a good road to be entranced by the sensation of life and power. To prove the extraordinary powers of endurance and economy which the machine of to-day possesses the Auto-Cycle Union, which rules the motor-cycle world, organised the road race at the Isle of Man last September. To the surprise of all, a single-cylinder machine won this event, averaging over forty miles an hour for 160 miles, and, what is more extraordinary still, its petrol consumption worked out at about 110 miles to a gallon. This shows how economically some machines run. It must be remembered that this was the severest possible test which could be imposed on a machine.

Many potential motor-cyclists are wondering how much it will cost them to run a machine. The answer is, it all depends on the machine. If, in the first place, they go in for a first-class make which has a reputation to uphold, their upkeep will be practically negligible, providing, of course, they always look after their mount themselves. Petrol and oil are the smallest items of all in a year's running expenses. Tyres are much better than they used to be, and a good strong pair of covers should last four or five thousand miles. The back tyre will wear out first, and it is advisable to change it over to the front wheel after two thousand miles. The next item of expense to consider would be the belt. Probably in a few years this will disappear altogether, and will give place to shaft drive of some sort. At present, however, it is standard on most machines. There are one or two notable exceptions. The belt, as has already been pointed out, is inclined to bespatter the rider with mud, and under some circumstances, especially when wet, is liable to slip—all this causes wear. The average life of a belt is about 1,800 miles. These are the only items that need replacing at set intervals, though, perhaps, a new sparking plug or valve might be requisitioned once every six months. The distance run is naturally the deciding factor in upkeep. Most motor-cyclists only use their machines at week-ends, averaging annually four or five thousand miles. A good machine will run this distance with one overhaul. This consists in taking the cylinder off and scraping away the burnt oil from the piston, regrinding the valves, and cleaning out the crank-case. All this can easily be done on a wet afternoon. To many people's minds, especially novices, this constitutes what is known as tuning up. Regarding depreciation, it is difficult to decide what is a fair price for a machine after, say, ten thousand miles. If it is only a year old it naturally fetches a better second-hand price than a three-year-old which has covered only half the distance. The writer was very lucky in disposing of his last machine to a syndicate for £40, and this after six thousand miles. The syndicate consists of two, who each paid half, but they find it difficult to decide who shall ride the motor next. The better plan is to get a whole machine.

For a man who is mechanically inclined a great deal of amusement may be got from owning one of these speedy little motors. He will soon learn all the intricacies of ignition and carburation, and, indeed, if he is thinking of going in for a motor-car later, he will get no better education in the peculiarities of the petrol engine than by studying his motor-cycle. Everyone who owns a motor-cycle is an enthusiast, and in many cases an expert also. Many experiments which afterwards become successful on motor-cars have owed their origin and upbringing to the humble motor-cycle. Many more have never come to light.

The writer well remembers when testing a carburetter with alcohol on the road being suddenly confronted by an obstinate cow, which had somehow got across his front wheel, with her fore legs on one side and her hind legs on the other. As she seemed firmly embedded on the front wheel it seemed rather hard to be requested by the yokel in charge to take the d——d motor-cycle off, and he calmly replied that he could not go until the yokel had first removed his d——d cow!

The improvements in the present-day models are many. The most noteworthy is what is known as handle-bar control. In old days the control of the engine was worked by levers from the tank, which constantly shook and automatically set themselves in all sorts of undesired positions. All this has now been done away with, and in its place there are two small levers on the handle-bar which can easily be worked by two fingers. There is no need now to let go of the handle-grip to alter the speed, and this is specially useful when on greasy roads, or when the local policeman unexpectedly appears. Everything on the modern machine is so much better made and so much stronger than it used to be. How seldom one sees a machine hung up on the roadside!

Some people will have it that the motor-cycle is going out. This seems absurd on the face of it, for at present there are over fifty-five thousand machines in this country used for pleasure purposes alone. Many firms who gave up making motor-cycles, have returned to their former love. A well-known company for the last two years have been very busy, and have continually, through winter and summer, been turning out sixty machines a week. At Brooklands, too, the management have seen fit to cultivate racing on these small two-wheelers, which have greatly attracted the public by tearing round the track at over seventy miles an hour.

The uses to which the ordinary machine can be put are very numerous. It can be used for going to and from the golf course, and for getting away from one's work, if in town, at week-ends. There are many worse ways of spending a fortnight's holiday than by making a tour with a few kindred spirits on motor-cycles. The great thing to remember when on a trip of this sort is to see one's own country before going abroad, and not to plan to cover too great distances daily. Another point in favour of this means of locomotion is that, should anything unforeseen occur in the way of breakdowns or accidents, it is the simplest matter in the world to take off the belt, and pedal the machine to the nearest railway station, where the railway company will take it for twice the rate of an ordinary cycle. Not so with a motor-car, which, if it break down, must be left at the roadside, perhaps throughout the night, till the nearest expert arrives. The writer will be pleased to answer any questions on the subject, and hopes that some of his readers will be induced by these remarks to make or renew their acquaintance with this form of motor.